THE MUFFIN COOKBOOK

Muffins for All Occasions

PUBLICATIONS INTERNATIONAL, LTD.

This edition published by:
Publications International, Ltd.
7373 N. Cicero Avenue
Lincolnwood, IL 60646

Library of Congress Catalog Card Number: 89-62986

ISBN 0-7853-0050-3

Photo credits: Vuksanovich, Chicago, IL, pages 4-5, 9, 13, 18, 22-23, 29, 33, 36, 40, 44-45, 48, 51, 62-63, 66, 69, 73, 74, 77, 78, 80-81, 84, 91 and cover.

Pictured on front and back covers:

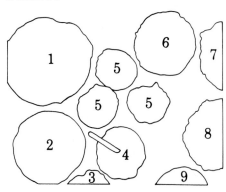

1. Crunch Top Blueberry Muffin (page 46)
2. Pineapple Carrot Raisin Muffins (page 60)
3. Chili Corn Muffin (page 75)
4. Taffy Apple Muffin (page 46)
5. Herbed Parmesan Muffin (page 27)
6. Orange Coconut Muffin (page 90)
7. Tropical Treat Muffin (page 85)
8. Whole Wheat Herb Muffin (page 24)
9. Honey Muffin (page 76)
10. Streusel Raspberry Muffin (page 82)
11. Turkey Ham, Cheese & Pepper Muffin (page 28)
12. Calico Bell Pepper Muffin (page 41)

Manufactured in USA

h g f e d c b a

Nutrition information is given for some of the recipes in this book. This information was computed for the food items in the ingredient list. When more than one ingredient choice is listed, the first ingredient was used for analysis. Optional and serve with ingredients are not included in the analysis. Numbers may have been rounded off.

THE MUFFIN COOKBOOK

Muffins for All Occasions

Microwave cooking times in this book are approximate. Numerous variables, such as the microwave oven's rated wattage and the starting temperature, shape, amount and depth of the food, can affect cooking time. Use the cooking times as a guideline and check doneness before adding more time. Lower wattage ovens may consistently require longer cooking times.

GREAT-START
MUFFINS

Muffins are a great way to start the day! The aroma of freshly baked muffins will be sure to entice the family out of bed. Muffins complement eggs, fruit or a morning beverage. They can be easily eaten while dressing or commuting to work or school. Pictured here are Nutty Banana Jam Muffins and Peanut Orange Breakfast Puffs. See page 6 for recipes.

Nutty Banana Jam Muffins

These muffins have a sweet surprise in the center.

1¼ cups ground walnuts
1½ cups sugar
¾ cup butter or margarine, softened
2 extra-ripe, medium DOLE™ Bananas, peeled
1 egg
2 cups all-purpose flour

2 teaspoons baking powder
1½ teaspoons ground cinnamon
½ teaspoon ground nutmeg
¼ teaspoon salt
1 ripe, small DOLE™ Banana, peeled
3 tablespoons raspberry jam

Line 18 (2½-inch) muffin cups with paper liners. In shallow dish, combine ¾ cup walnuts with ½ cup sugar; set aside.

In large bowl, beat remaining ½ cup nuts with remaining 1 cup sugar and butter until light and fluffy. Puree 2 medium bananas in blender (1 cup). Beat pureed bananas and egg into sugar-butter mixture. In medium bowl, combine flour, baking powder, cinnamon, nutmeg and salt. Beat dry ingredients into banana mixture until well mixed.

Mash small banana in small bowl; stir in raspberry jam. For each muffin, roll 1 heaping tablespoon dough in walnut-sugar mixture to coat. Place in lined muffin cup. Make a dimple in center of dough with back of spoon. Spoon 1 teaspoon jam mixture into center. Roll 1 more heaping tablespoon dough in walnut-sugar mixture. Drop over jam mixture. Repeat with remaining dough and jam mixture.

Bake in 400° oven 15 to 20 minutes or until wooden pick inserted in center comes out clean. Cool slightly in pan; cool slightly on wire rack. Serve warm.

Makes 18 muffins

Peanut Orange Breakfast Puffs

2 cups sifted all-purpose flour
1 tablespoon baking powder
1 teaspoon salt
¼ cup sugar

1 egg, beaten
1 cup milk
¼ cup peanut oil
½ cup chopped salted peanuts

Topping:
¼ cup sugar
1 teaspoon grated orange peel

¼ cup butter or margarine, melted

In large bowl, sift together flour, baking powder, salt and ¼ cup sugar. In small bowl, combine egg, milk and peanut oil. Add liquid all at once to flour mixture, stirring only until moistened. Fold in chopped peanuts. Fill oiled 2½-inch muffin cups ⅔ full. Bake in preheated 425° oven 15 to 20 minutes or until tops are lightly browned. Meanwhile, in small bowl, blend ¼ cup sugar and orange peel until crumbly. When muffins are baked, remove from muffin cups and immediately dip tops in melted butter, then in orange-sugar mixture. Serve warm. *Makes 12 muffins*

Favorite recipe from **Oklahoma Peanut Commission**

Banana Blueberry Muffins

2 extra-ripe, medium DOLE™
  Bananas, peeled
2 eggs
1 cup packed brown sugar
½ cup butter or margarine, melted
1 cup blueberries

1 teaspoon vanilla
2¼ cups all-purpose flour
2 teaspoons baking powder
½ teaspoon ground cinnamon
½ teaspoon salt

Puree bananas in blender (1 cup). In medium bowl, combine bananas, eggs, sugar and butter until well blended. Stir in blueberries and vanilla. In large bowl, combine flour, baking powder, cinnamon and salt. Stir banana mixture into flour mixture until evenly moistened. Spoon batter into well greased 2½-inch muffin cups. Bake in 350° oven 25 to 30 minutes or until wooden pick inserted in center comes out clean. Serve warm. *Makes 12 muffins*

Banana Blueberry Muffins

Bacon-Cheese Muffins

½ pound bacon (10 to 12 slices)
Vegetable oil
1 egg, beaten
¾ cup milk
1¾ cups all-purpose flour

¼ cup sugar
1 tablespoon baking powder
1 cup (4 ounces) shredded
    Wisconsin Cheddar cheese
½ cup crunchy nugget-like cereal

In large skillet, cook bacon over medium-high heat until crisp. Drain, reserving drippings. If necessary, add oil to drippings to measure ⅓ cup. In small bowl, combine dripping mixture, egg and milk; set aside. Crumble bacon; set aside.

In large bowl, combine flour, sugar and baking powder. Make well in center. Add dripping-egg mixture all at once to flour mixture, stirring just until moistened. Batter should be lumpy. Fold in bacon, cheese and cereal. Spoon into greased or paper-lined 2½-inch muffin cups, filling about ¾ full. Bake in preheated 400° oven 15 to 20 minutes or until golden. Remove from pan. Cool on wire rack.

Makes 12 muffins

Favorite recipe from **Wisconsin Milk Marketing Board**© 1989

Strawberry Muffins

1¼ cups all-purpose flour
2½ teaspoons baking powder
½ teaspoon salt
1 cup uncooked rolled oats
½ cup sugar

1 cup milk
½ cup butter or margarine, melted
1 egg, beaten
1 teaspoon vanilla extract
1 cup chopped strawberries

Preheat oven to 425°. Grease 12 (2½-inch) muffin-pan cups; set aside. In large bowl, sift together flour, baking powder and salt. Stir in rolled oats and sugar. Make well in center. In small bowl, combine milk, butter, egg and vanilla. Pour into flour mixture, stirring just until flour mixture is moistened. Fold in strawberries. Spoon into muffin cups, filling each about ⅔ full. Bake 15 to 18 minutes or until lightly brown and toothpick inserted in centers comes out clean. Remove from pan.

Makes 12 muffins

Bacon-Cheese Muffins

Sausage Corn Muffins

½ pound ECKRICH® Smoked   1 tablespoon baking powder
    Sausage ·   1 cup buttermilk
1 cup unsifted all-purpose flour   ¼ cup vegetable oil
¾ cup yellow cornmeal   2 eggs, beaten
¼ cup sugar   Honey Butter (recipe follows)

Preheat oven to 375°. Cut sausage into quarters lengthwise, then cut crosswise into ¼-inch pieces. Lightly brown sausage in medium skillet over medium heat. Drain on paper towels. Combine flour, cornmeal, sugar and baking powder in medium bowl. Add buttermilk, oil, eggs and sausage. Stir only until blended. Fill paper-lined 2½-inch muffin cups ⅔ full. Bake 12 to 15 minutes or until wooden pick inserted near center comes out clean. Serve with Honey Butter.   *Makes 15 muffins*

Honey Butter: Blend ½ cup softened butter or margarine and ¼ cup honey in small bowl.

Sausage Corn Muffins

Morning Muffins

2¾ cups QUAKER® Crunchy Bran
    Cereal finely crushed to 1 cup
1½ cups all-purpose flour
⅓ cup packed brown sugar
4 teaspoons baking powder

1 teaspoon ground cinnamon
1 cup chopped pitted prunes
1¼ cups 2% low-fat milk
⅓ cup vegetable oil
1 egg

Heat oven to 400°. Grease or paper-line 12 (2½-inch) muffin cups. In large bowl, combine cereal, flour, brown sugar, baking powder and cinnamon. Stir in prunes. In small bowl, combine milk, oil and egg. Add to flour mixture, stirring just until moistened. Fill muffin cups almost full. Bake 25 minutes or until wooden pick inserted in center comes out clean. Cool in pan on wire rack 5 minutes. Remove from pan. Cool on wire rack.   *Makes 12 muffins*

Tips

To freeze muffins: Wrap securely in foil or place in freezer bag. Seal, label and freeze.

To reheat frozen muffins: Unwrap muffins; wrap in paper towel. Microwave at HIGH (100%) about 45 seconds per muffin.

Nutrition information: Each serving (1 muffin)
Calories 230, Dietary Fiber 3 g

Lemony Apple Oat Muffins

1¼ cups unsifted flour
½ cup packed light brown sugar
1½ teaspoons baking powder
1 teaspoon baking soda
1 teaspoon ground cinnamon
½ teaspoon salt
¼ teaspoon ground nutmeg
1 egg
½ cup BORDEN® or MEADOW
    GOLD® Milk

¼ cup vegetable oil
2 tablespoons REALEMON® Lemon
    Juice from Concentrate
¾ cup quick-cooking oats
1 cup finely chopped all-purpose
    apples
½ cup chopped nuts
    Lemon Glaze (recipe follows)

Preheat oven to 400°. In small bowl, combine flour, sugar, baking powder, baking soda, cinnamon, salt and nutmeg. In medium bowl, beat egg; stir in milk, oil, then ReaLemon® brand. Add oats; mix well. Add flour mixture, apples and nuts; stir only until moistened (batter will be thick). Spoon into greased or paper-lined 2½-inch muffin cups. Bake 20 minutes or until golden. Spoon Lemon Glaze over muffins. Remove from pans; serve warm.   *Makes about 12 muffins*

Lemon Glaze: In small bowl, combine ½ cup confectioners' sugar, 1 tablespoon ReaLemon® brand and 1 tablespoon melted margarine or butter. Makes about ¼ cup.

Cranberry Banana Muffins

Tart cranberries and ripened, sweet bananas provide an extra twist to the traditional oat bran muffin.

2 cups QUAKER OAT BRAN™ Hot
    Cereal, uncooked
½ cup packed brown sugar
¼ cup all-purpose flour
2 teaspoons baking powder
½ teaspoon salt (optional)
½ teaspoon ground cinnamon

½ cup finely chopped cranberries
⅔ cup cranberry juice cocktail
½ cup mashed ripe banana (about
    1 medium)
2 egg whites, slightly beaten
3 tablespoons vegetable oil

Heat oven to 400°. Paper-line 12 (2½-inch) muffin cups. In large bowl, combine oat bran, brown sugar, flour, baking powder, salt and cinnamon. Gently stir in cranberries. In small bowl, combined cranberry juice, banana, egg whites and oil. Stir into flour mixture, mixing just until moistened. Fill muffin cups almost full. Bake 20 to 22 minutes or until golden brown and wooden pick inserted in center comes out clean. Remove from pan. *Makes 12 muffins*

Tips

To freeze muffins: Wrap securely in foil or place in freezer bag. Seal, label and freeze.

To reheat frozen muffins: Unwrap muffins. Microwave at HIGH (100%) about 30 seconds per muffin.

Nutrition information: Each serving (1 muffin)
Calories 150, Protein 4 g, Carbohydrate 24 g, Fat 5 g (polyunsaturated 2 g, monounsaturated 2 g, saturated 0 g), Oat Bran 14 g, Dietary Fiber 2 g, Sodium 85 mg, Cholesterol 0 mg
Percentage of calories from fat: 28%, Diabetic exchanges: 1 Starch/Bread; 1 Fat; ½ Fruit

Cheesy Bacon 'n Apple Muffins

2 cups sifted all-purpose flour
¼ cup sugar
4 teaspoons baking powder
¾ teaspoon salt
1 cup milk
⅓ cup butter, melted
1 egg, slightly beaten

½ cup finely chopped unpeeled
    apple
¾ cup (3 ounces) shredded aged
    Cheddar cheese
⅔ cup crisp bacon crumbles (about
    8 slices)

In large bowl, sift together flour, sugar, baking powder and salt. In small bowl, combine milk, butter and egg; stir into dry ingredients just until moistened. Fold in apple, cheese and bacon crumbles. Spoon into buttered muffin cups, filling ⅔ full. Bake in preheated 400° oven 15 to 20 minutes or until golden brown. Remove from pan. Cool on wire rack. *Makes 18 muffins*

Favorite recipe from **Wisconsin Milk Marketing Board© 1989**

Cranberry Banana Muffins

Bountiful Breakfast Muffins

1 cup all-purpose flour
1 teaspoon baking powder
¼ teaspoon pumpkin pie spice
1 cup (4 ounces) prepackaged diced
    mixed dried fruit bits

½ cup butter, softened
⅔ cup sugar
6 eggs
1 teaspoon vanilla
⅓ cup rolled oats

In small bowl, stir together flour, baking powder and spice. Toss fruit with 1 tablespoon of the flour mixture. Set both mixtures aside.

In large bowl, beat at medium speed, butter and sugar until light and fluffy. Beat in eggs until well blended. Beat in vanilla. At low speed, gradually beat in reserved flour mixture just until blended. Stir in reserved fruit and oats.

Line 12 (2½-inch) muffin cups with paper baking cups. Pour a scant ⅓ cup batter into each cup. Bake in preheated 350° oven 20 minutes or until wooden pick inserted in center comes out clean. Remove from pan. Cool on wire rack.

Makes 12 muffins

Favorite recipe from **American Egg Board**

Bountiful Breakfast Muffins

Pumpkin Bran Muffins

1 cup wheat bran cereal (not flaked)
½ cup *undiluted* CARNATION®
   Evaporated Milk
1¼ cups all-purpose flour
⅔ cup sugar
1 tablespoon baking powder
1 teaspoon ground cinnamon
½ teaspoon salt

½ teaspoon ground nutmeg
¼ teaspoon ground cloves
1 cup LIBBY'S® Solid Pack
   Pumpkin
½ cup vegetable oil
1 egg, slightly beaten
½ cup raisins
3 tablespoons cinnamon-sugar

In medium bowl, combine cereal and milk. Let stand 10 minutes or until milk is absorbed. In large bowl, combine flour, sugar, baking powder, cinnamon, salt, nutmeg and cloves; set aside. Add pumpkin, oil, egg and raisins to cereal. Add liquid ingredients to dry ingredients; stir just until moistened. Spoon batter into greased or paper-lined 2½-inch muffin cups, filling to top. Sprinkle each muffin with 1 teaspoon cinnamon-sugar. Bake in preheated 400° oven for 25 to 30 minutes or until wooden pick inserted in center comes out clean. Cool in pan on wire rack 3 to 4 minutes. Remove from pan; cool on wire rack. *Makes 9 muffins*

Oatmeal Raisin Muffins

1 can (8 ounces) DOLE® Crushed
   Pineapple
1 cup dairy sour cream
1 egg
¼ cup butter or margarine, melted
1½ cups all-purpose flour
1 cup old-fashioned oats

½ cup sugar
1 tablespoon baking powder
1 teaspoon ground cinnamon
½ teaspoon ground nutmeg
½ teaspoon salt
1 cup DOLE™ Raisins

In small bowl, combine undrained pineapple, sour cream, egg and butter until blended. In large bowl, combine remaining ingredients; make well in center. Pour in pineapple mixture. Stir until just mixed. Spoon into greased 2½-inch muffin cups. Bake in 350° oven 30 to 35 minutes until lightly browned and wooden pick inserted in center comes out clean. Serve warm. *Makes 12 muffins*

Breakfast Muffins

These have a hearty texture and a nut-like flavor.

1¾ cups sifted all-purpose flour
2 tablespoons sugar
1 teaspoon baking powder
½ teaspoon ARM & HAMMER®
    Baking Soda

½ teaspoon salt
1 cup buttermilk
1 egg, slightly beaten
3 tablespoons butter or margarine,
    melted

In large bowl, sift together flour, sugar, baking powder, baking soda and salt. In medium bowl, combine buttermilk, egg and butter. Pour into flour mixture, stirring just until moistened. Spoon into greased 2½-inch muffin cups, filling ⅔ full. Bake in 400° oven 20 to 25 minutes. Remove from pan. Serve warm with butter or preserves.

Makes about 12 muffins

Banana-Bran Muffins

¾ cup wheat bran cereal
¼ cup milk
2 extra-ripe, medium DOLE®
    Bananas, peeled and sliced
1 egg
¼ cup light molasses

2 tablespoons vegetable oil
1 cup all-purpose flour
1 teaspoon baking soda
¼ teaspoon salt
¾ cup DOLE® Raisins

Preheat oven to 375°. Grease 6 muffin-pan cups; set aside. In small bowl, combine cereal and milk; let stand 10 minutes. In covered blender or food processor, puree bananas. In medium bowl, combine bananas, egg, molasses and oil until well blended. In another small bowl, combine flour, baking soda and salt. Stir cereal mixture and flour mixture into banana mixture just until flour mixture is moistened. Batter will be lumpy. Fold in raisins. Spoon into muffin cups, filling each about ⅔ full. Bake 25 to 28 minutes or until toothpick inserted in centers comes out clean. Remove from pan; serve warm.

Makes 6 muffins

Peanut Butter Bran Muffins

½ cup peanut butter
2 tablespoons butter or margarine
¼ cup packed brown sugar
1 egg
1 cup wheat bran cereal

1 cup milk
¾ cup all-purpose flour
1 tablespoon baking powder
½ teaspoon salt
½ cup raisins

Preheat oven to 400°. Grease 12 muffin-pan cups; set aside. In medium bowl, beat peanut butter, butter, sugar and egg until well blended. Stir in cereal and milk.

In large bowl, combine flour, baking powder and salt. Make well in center. Pour cereal mixture into flour mixture, stirring just until flour mixture is moistened. Batter will be lumpy. Fold in raisins. Spoon into muffin cups, filling each about ⅔ full. Bake 20 to 25 minutes or until golden and toothpick inserted in centers comes out clean. Remove from pan; serve warm. *Makes 12 muffins*

Golden Oat Muffins

1¼ cups all-purpose flour
1 tablespoon baking powder
1 cup uncooked rolled oats
1 container (8 ounces)
  MOUNTAIN HIGH® or
  BORDEN® LITE-LINE®
  Plain Yogurt

¾ cup CARY'S®, VERMONT MAPLE
  ORCHARDS or MACDONALD'S
  Pure Maple Syrup
¼ cup butter or margarine, melted
1 egg, lightly beaten
½ cup raisins
  Pecan halves

Preheat oven to 400°. Grease or paper-line 12 muffin-pan cups; set aside. In large bowl, combine flour and baking powder. Make well in center. In medium bowl, combine oats and yogurt; let stand 5 minutes. Stir in syrup, butter, egg and raisins; mix well. Pour into flour mixture, stirring just until flour mixture is moistened. Batter will be lumpy. Spoon into prepared muffin cups, filling each about ⅔ full. Top with pecan halves. Bake 20 to 25 minutes or until golden brown and toothpick inserted in centers comes out clean. Cool 5 minutes in pan on wire rack. Remove from pan; serve warm. *Makes about 12 muffins*

Blueberry Yogurt Muffins

Blueberry Yogurt Muffins

Try these moist, flourless yogurt muffins sweetened with the natural taste of honey and blueberry.

2 cups QUAKER OAT BRAN™ Hot
   Cereal, uncooked
¼ cup packed brown sugar
2 teaspoons baking powder
1 carton (8 ounces) plain low fat
   yogurt

2 egg whites, slightly beaten
¼ cup skim milk
¼ cup honey
2 tablespoons vegetable oil
1 teaspoon grated lemon peel
½ cup fresh or frozen blueberries

Heat oven to 425°. Paper-line 12 (2½-inch) muffin cups. In large bowl, combine oat bran, brown sugar and baking powder. In small bowl, combine yogurt, egg whites, skim milk, honey, oil and lemon peel. Stir into oat bran mixture, mixing just until moistened. Fold in blueberries. Fill muffin cups almost full. Bake 18 to 20 minutes or until golden brown and wooden pick inserted in center comes out clean. Remove from pan. *Makes 12 muffins*

Tips

To freeze muffins: Wrap securely in foil or place in freezer bag. Seal, label and freeze.

To reheat frozen muffins: Unwrap muffins. Microwave at HIGH (100%) about 30 seconds per muffin.

Nutrition information: Each serving (1 muffin)
Calories 130, Protein 5 g, Carbohydrate 21 g, Fat 4 g (polyunsaturated 2 g, monounsaturated 1 g, saturated 1 g), Oat Bran 14 g, Dietary Fiber 2 g, Sodium 100 mg, Cholesterol 0 mg
Percentage of calories from fat: 25%, Diabetic exchanges: 1 Starch/Bread; ½ Fruit; ½ Fat

Orange Glazed Muffins

1½ cups all-purpose flour
½ cup KRETSCHMER® Original or
   Honey Crunch Wheat Germ
¼ cup granulated sugar
1 tablespoon baking powder
1 tablespoon grated orange peel

½ teaspoon salt (optional)
⅔ cup milk
⅓ cup margarine, melted
2 eggs
½ cup powdered sugar
1 tablespoon orange juice

Heat oven to 400°. Grease or paper-line 12 (2½-inch) muffin cups. In large bowl, combine flour, wheat germ, granulated sugar, baking powder, orange peel and salt. In small bowl, combine milk, margarine and eggs. Add to flour mixture, stirring just until moistened. Fill muffin cups ⅔ full. Bake 20 to 25 minutes or until light golden brown and wooden pick inserted in center comes out clean. Remove from pan. Cool on wire rack. In small bowl, combine powdered sugar and orange juice. Drizzle over slightly cooled muffins. *Makes 12 muffins*

Blueberry Buttermilk Muffins

1 cup buttermilk
½ cup butter or margarine, melted
2 eggs, beaten
2½ cups all-purpose flour
1 cup sugar

2½ teaspoons baking powder
¼ teaspoon salt
1½ cups fresh or dry-pack frozen
    blueberries

In small bowl, combine buttermilk, butter and eggs until blended. In large bowl, combine flour, sugar, baking powder and salt. Make well in center. Add buttermilk mixture, stirring until flour mixture is just moistened. Fold in blueberries. Spoon batter into greased muffin cups, filling ⅔ full. Bake in preheated 400° oven 20 minutes or until tops are golden and wooden pick inserted in center comes out clean. Remove from pan. Serve warm or cool on wire rack.   *Makes about 18 muffins*

Favorite recipe from **MBG Marketing**™

Orange Pineapple Muffins

1 can (8 oz.) DOLE® Crushed
    Pineapple
1¾ cups all-purpose flour
¼ cup packed brown sugar
2 teaspoons baking powder
½ teaspoon salt

2 eggs, slightly beaten
¾ cup milk
3 tablespoons butter or margarine,
    melted
½ cup chopped walnuts
2 teaspoons grated orange peel

Drain pineapple. In large bowl, combine flour, sugar, baking powder and salt. In small bowl, combine eggs, milk and butter. Stir in pineapple, nuts and orange peel. Make well in center of dry ingredients. Pour in milk mixture. Stir just until moistened. Spoon into greased 2½-inch muffin cups. Bake in 400° oven 20 to 25 minutes or until wooden pick inserted in center comes out clean. Serve warm.

Makes 16 muffins

Date-Nut Muffins

What a way to start off the day! Moist muffins chock full of dates and nuts.

1 package (8 ounces) pitted dates,
    coarsely chopped
¾ cup boiling water
¼ cup MAZOLA® corn oil
½ teaspoon vanilla

1 cup all-purpose flour
½ cup whole wheat flour
½ cup sugar
⅓ cup coarsely chopped walnuts
½ teaspoon baking soda

In large bowl, combine dates, water, oil and vanilla; stir to mix. In medium bowl, combine flours, sugar, walnuts and baking soda. Add to date mixture, stirring just until moistened. Spoon into 12 greased 2½-inch muffin cups. Bake in preheated 375° oven 25 minutes or until wooden pick inserted in center comes out clean. Remove from pan. Serve warm or cool on wire rack.   *Makes 12 muffins*

Banana Poppy Seed Muffins

2 ripe, medium DOLE™ Bananas, peeled
1 egg
¾ cup sugar
¼ cup vegetable oil
2 teaspoons grated orange peel

2 cups all-purpose flour
1½ tablespoons poppy seeds
2 teaspoons baking powder
½ teaspoon salt
Citrus Glaze (recipe follows)

Puree bananas in blender (1 cup). In medium bowl, mix bananas, egg, sugar, oil and orange peel until well blended. In large bowl, combine flour, poppy seeds, baking powder and salt. Stir banana mixture into flour mixture until evenly moistened. Spoon batter into greased 2½-inch muffin cups. Bake in 375° oven 20 minutes or until wooden pick inserted in center comes out clean. Remove from pan; cool on wire rack. Top with Citrus Glaze while warm. *Makes 12 muffins*

Citrus Glaze: In medium bowl, combine 1¼ cups powdered sugar, ¼ cup orange juice, 1 teaspoon grated orange peel and 1 teaspoon vanilla until smooth.

Banana Poppy Seed Muffins

SAVORY
M U F F I N S

Savory muffins have a hearty flavor and make a
delightful side dish to any meal. Herbs, cheese, vegetables,
fruits and grains are used to create
wonderful tasting muffins. Serve with soup
and a salad for a light lunch or as an accompaniment for
dinner. Pictured here are Whole Wheat
Herb Muffins and Wisconsin Blue Cheese Muffins.
See page 24 for recipes.

Whole Wheat Herb Muffins

1 cup all-purpose flour
1 cup whole wheat flour
⅓ cup sugar
2 teaspoons baking powder
½ teaspoon baking soda
½ teaspoon salt
½ teaspoon dried basil leaves
¼ teaspoon dried marjoram leaves
¼ teaspoon dried oregano leaves
⅛ teaspoon dried thyme leaves
¾ cup raisins
1 cup buttermilk
2 tablespoons butter or margarine, melted
1 egg, beaten
2 tablespoons wheat germ

Preheat oven to 400°. Grease 12 (2½-inch) muffin cups. In large bowl, combine flours, sugar, baking powder, baking soda, salt, herbs and raisins. In small bowl, combine buttermilk, butter and egg. Stir into flour mixture just until moistened. Spoon into muffin cups. Sprinkle wheat germ on tops. Bake 15 to 20 minutes or until lightly browned and wooden pick inserted in center comes out clean. Remove from pan. *Makes 12 muffins*

Wisconsin Blue Cheese Muffins

Blue cheese lovers beware! This muffin could be addicting. The golden exterior and the nuggets of melted cheese make these muffins hard to resist.

2 cups all-purpose flour
3 tablespoons sugar
1 tablespoon baking powder
¼ teaspoon salt
1 cup Wisconsin Blue Cheese, crumbled
1 egg, beaten
1 cup milk
¼ cup butter, melted

Preheat oven to 400°. Butter 2½-inch muffin cups. In large bowl, combine flour, sugar, baking powder, salt and cheese. In small bowl, combine egg, milk and butter until blended. Stir into flour mixture just until moistened. Spoon into muffin cups, filling ¾ full. Bake 20 to 25 minutes or until golden brown. Remove from pan; serve warm. *Makes 10 muffins*

Favorite recipe from **Wisconsin Milk Marketing Board© 1989.**

Country Corn Muffins

2 (8½-ounce) packages corn muffin mix
10 slices bacon, cooked and crumbled
¾ cup BAMA® Strawberry or Blackberry Preserves

Preheat oven to 400°. Prepare muffin mix according to package directions; stir in bacon. Fill paper-lined 2½-inch muffin cups ⅓ full. Drop 2 level teaspoons preserves in center of each. Add remaining batter to fill cups ¾ full. Bake 15 to 20 minutes or until golden brown. Remove from pans. Serve warm. *Makes 12 to 18 muffins*

Tex-Mex Pumpkin Corn Muffins

1 cup yellow cornmeal
1 cup all-purpose flour
2 tablespoons sugar
4 teaspoons baking powder
½ teaspoon salt
½ teaspoon chili powder
2 eggs
1 cup LIBBY'S® Solid Pack
    Pumpkin

1 cup milk
2 tablespoons vegetable oil
1 can (4 ounces) chopped green
    chilies
¾ cup (3 ounces) shredded Cheddar
    cheese

In large bowl, combine cornmeal, flour, sugar, baking powder, salt and chili powder.
In small bowl, beat eggs; mix in pumpkin, milk, oil and chiles. Add pumpkin mixture
to flour mixture; stir just until moistened. Spoon into 18 greased or paper-lined 2½-
inch muffin cups. Sprinkle with cheese. Bake in preheated 400° oven for 20 to 25
minutes or until wooden pick inserted in center comes out clean. Remove from pan.
Serve warm.   *Makes 18 muffins*

Note: Batter may be baked in any of the following well-greased pans, in preheated
425° oven for 20 to 25 minutes or until wooden pick inserted in center comes out
clean. To avoid sticking, be sure cheese is not too close to edges of pan.
    One 10-inch cast iron skillet
    Two 9-inch divided metal pans
    Corn-stick pans (omit cheese on top)

Tex-Mex Pumpkin Corn Muffins with Corn Stick and Corn Bread variations

Popover Pan Muffins

2 cups all-purpose flour
¾ cup sugar
2 teaspoons pumpkin pie spice
¾ teaspoon baking powder
¾ teaspoon baking soda
¾ teaspoon salt

3 eggs
¾ cup almond oil
2 teaspoons vanilla
1 cup grated zucchini
½ cup chopped toasted almonds
½ cup seedless raisins

Preheat oven to 375°. Grease 6 popover pans.* In large bowl, combine flour, sugar, pumpkin pie spice, baking powder, baking soda and salt. In small bowl, beat eggs with oil and vanilla. Add to flour mixture with zucchini, almonds and raisins. Stir just until moistened. Spoon into popover pans. Bake in center of oven 25 minutes.

Makes 6 popover pan muffins

*To make standard-size muffins, divide batter among 18 (2½-inch) muffin cups. Bake in a preheated 375° oven 20 minutes.   *Makes 18 muffins*

Favorite recipe from **Almond Board of California**

Popover Pan Muffins

Apple-Cranberry Muffins

1¾ cups plus 2 tablespoons all-purpose flour
½ cup sugar
1½ teaspoons baking powder
½ teaspoon baking soda
½ teaspoon salt
1 egg

¾ cup milk
¾ cup sweetened applesauce
¼ cup butter or margarine, melted
1 cup fresh cranberries, coarsely chopped
½ teaspoon ground cinnamon

In medium bowl, combine 1¾ cups of the flour, ¼ cup of the sugar, the baking powder, baking soda and salt. In small bowl, combine egg, milk, applesauce and butter; mix well. Add egg mixture to flour mixture, stirring just until moistened. Batter will be lumpy. In small bowl, toss cranberries with remaining 2 tablespoons flour; fold into batter. Spoon batter into 12 greased 2½-inch muffin cups. In another small bowl, combine remaining ¼ cup sugar and the cinnamon. Sprinkle over muffins. Bake in preheated 400° oven 20 to 25 minutes or until wooden pick inserted in center comes out clean. Remove from pan; cool on wire rack.

Makes 12 muffins

Favorite recipe from **Western New York Apple Growers Association, Inc.**

Herbed Parmesan Muffins

Serve these muffins with an Italian-style meal or a minestrone soup.

2 cups all-purpose flour
¾ cup grated Parmesan cheese
2 teaspoons sugar
2 teaspoons baking powder
2 teaspoons mixed Italian-style herb seasoning*
½ teaspoon baking soda

½ teaspoon salt
½ cup chopped fresh basil, parsley or cilantro leaves
1¼ cups buttermilk
¼ cup olive or vegetable oil
1 egg

Preheat oven to 400°. Grease bottoms only of 12 (2½-inch) or 36 miniature muffin cups. In large bowl, combine flour, Parmesan, sugar, baking powder, herb seasoning, baking soda, salt and basil. In small bowl, combine buttermilk, oil and egg until blended. Stir into flour mixture just until moistened. Spoon into muffin cups. Bake 15 to 20 minutes for regular-size muffins, 12 to 15 minutes for miniature muffins or until golden and wooden pick inserted in center comes out clean. Remove from pan. Serve warm.

Makes 12 regular-size or 36 miniature muffins

*Italian-style herb seasoning is a blend of marjoram, thyme, rosemary, savory, sage, oregano and basil.

Spiced Brown Bread Muffins

Quick to make, serve these with a hearty stew.

2 cups whole wheat flour
⅔ cup all-purpose flour
⅔ cup packed brown sugar
2 teaspoons baking soda

1 teaspoon pumpkin pie spice
2 cups buttermilk
¾ cup raisins

Preheat oven to 350°. Grease 6 (4-inch) muffin cups. In large bowl, combine flours, sugar, baking soda and pumpkin pie spice. Stir in buttermilk just until flour mixture is moistened. Fold in raisins. Spoon into muffin cups. Bake 35 to 40 minutes or until wooden pick inserted in center comes out clean. Remove from pan.

Makes 6 giant muffins

Turkey Ham, Cheese & Pepper Muffins

Serve these savory muffins baked in miniature muffin cups as an appetizer. Larger muffins are a perfect accompaniment to salad or soup.

¼ cup butter or margarine
½ cup minced sweet onion
¼ cup minced green bell pepper
1 clove garlic, minced or pressed
2 cups all-purpose flour
1 tablespoon baking powder
1 teaspoon salt
½ teaspoon coarsely ground black pepper

1 cup milk
2 eggs
1 cup (4 ounces) finely diced turkey ham
½ cup diced Cheddar cheese
¼ cup roasted shelled sunflower seeds

Preheat oven to 375°. Generously grease or paper-line 12 (2½-inch) or 36 miniature muffin cups. In heavy skillet, over medium-high heat, melt butter. Add onion, green pepper and garlic; cook and stir 5 to 7 minutes or until onion is translucent.

In large bowl, combine flour, baking powder, salt and pepper. In small bowl, combine milk and eggs until blended. Add milk mixture, vegetables with drippings, turkey and cheese to flour mixture. Stir mixture just until moistened. Spoon into muffin cups. Sprinkle sunflower seeds over tops. Bake 25 to 30 minutes for regular-size muffins, 15 to 20 minutes for miniature muffins or until wooden pick inserted in center comes out clean. Remove from pan.

Makes 12 regular-size muffins or 36 miniature muffins

Spiced Brown Bread Muffins

Top: Fruited Corn Muffins Bottom: Orange Spice Muffins

Orange Spice Muffins

⅓ cup packed brown sugar
¼ cup margarine or butter, softened
1 egg, beaten
¾ cup BORDEN® or MEADOW
   GOLD® Milk
½ cup orange juice
1 tablespoon grated orange peel

3 cups biscuit baking mix
1 (9-ounce) package NONE SUCH®
   Condensed Mincemeat,
   crumbled
Cinnamon and Sugar Topping
   (recipe follows)

Preheat oven to 375°. In large bowl, beat sugar and margarine until fluffy. Add egg, milk, orange juice and peel; mix well. Stir in biscuit mix and mincemeat only until moistened (do not overmix). Fill greased or paper-lined 2½-inch muffin cups ¾ full. Sprinkle Cinnamon and Sugar Topping evenly over muffins. Bake 18 to 22 minutes or until golden brown. Remove from pan. Serve warm.   *Makes about 18 muffins*

Cinnamon and Sugar Topping: In small bowl, combine 2 tablespoons sugar and 2 teaspoons ground cinnamon.

Fruited Corn Muffins

2 (8½-ounce) packages *or*
  1 (18-ounce) package corn
  muffin mix

1 (9-ounce) package NONE SUCH®
  Condensed Mincemeat, finely
  crumbled

Preheat oven to 400°. Prepare muffin mix according to package directions, stirring in mincemeat. Fill greased or paper-lined 2½-inch muffin cups ½ full. Bake 15 to 18 minutes or until golden brown. Remove from pan. Serve warm.

Makes about 18 muffins

Mandarin Muffins

1 can (8¼ ounces) DOLE® Crushed
  Pineapple
  Milk
2 cups all-purpose flour
⅓ cup packed brown sugar
2 tablespoons toasted wheat germ
1 tablespoon baking powder

½ teaspoon salt
1 egg, beaten
¾ cup finely shredded carrot
⅓ cup vegetable oil
½ teaspoon vanilla
2 tablespoons granulated sugar
½ teaspoon ground cinnamon

Drain pineapple well, reserving syrup. (Press pineapple with back of spoon to remove as much syrup as possible.) Add enough milk to syrup to measure ¾ cup liquid.

In large bowl, combine flour, brown sugar, wheat germ, baking powder and salt. Make well in center. In medium bowl, combine egg, carrot, oil, vanilla, milk-syrup mixture and pineapple. Add pineapple mixture all at once to dry ingredients, stirring just until moistened. Batter should be lumpy. Fill paper-lined 2½-inch muffin cups ⅔ full. In small bowl, combine granulated sugar and cinnamon; sprinkle over tops of muffins. Bake in 400° oven 20 to 25 minutes or until wooden pick inserted in center comes out clean. Remove from pan.

Makes 15 muffins

Herb Cheese Muffins

Herbed cream cheese is soft and spreadable, available in the deli section of your supermarket. These muffins are great served with any chicken breast or fish dish.

1½ cups all-purpose flour
2 teaspoons baking powder
½ teaspoon salt
¼ teaspoon freshly ground black
  pepper
⅔ cup milk

1 package (4 ounces) soft
  spreadable herbed cream
  cheese
1 egg, beaten
2 teaspoons minced fresh chives

Preheat oven to 375°. Grease or paper-line 12 (2½-inch) muffin cups. In large bowl, combine flour, baking powder, salt and black pepper. In small bowl, combine milk, cream cheese, egg and chives until blended. Stir into flour mixture just until moistened. Spoon into muffin cups. Bake 15 to 20 minutes or until wooden pick inserted in center comes out clean. Remove from pan. Serve warm.

Makes 12 muffins

Southern Biscuit Muffins

These muffins taste like baking powder biscuits and are very quick and easy to make. Serve them with jelly, jam or honey.

2½ cups all-purpose flour
¼ cup sugar
1½ tablespoons baking powder

¾ cup cold butter or margarine
1 cup cold milk

Preheat oven to 400°. Grease 12 (2½-inch) muffin cups. (These muffins brown better on the sides and bottom when baked without paper liners.) In large bowl, combine flour, sugar and baking powder. Cut in butter until mixture resembles coarse crumbs. Stir in milk just until flour mixture is moistened. Spoon into muffin cups. Bake 20 minutes or until golden. Remove from pan. Cool on wire rack.

Makes 12 muffins

Whole Wheat Muffins

¾ cup all-purpose flour
¾ cup whole wheat flour
2 teaspoons baking powder
½ teaspoon salt

1 egg
½ cup packed brown sugar
½ cup milk
½ cup vegetable oil

Preheat oven to 375°. Grease 2½-inch muffin cups; set aside. In large bowl, combine flours, baking powder and salt. Make well in center. In medium bowl, combine egg, sugar, milk and oil until well blended. Pour into flour mixture, stirring just until moistened. Spoon into muffin cups, filling ⅔ full. Bake 20 to 25 minutes or until wooden pick inserted in centers comes out clean. Remove from pan; serve warm.

Makes 12 muffins

Southern Biscuit Muffins

Honey-Lemon Muffins

¾ cup ROMAN MEAL® ORIGINAL
    WHEAT, RYE, BRAN, FLAX
    CEREAL
1½ cups all-purpose flour
1 tablespoon baking powder
½ teaspoon salt

1 egg, slightly beaten
1 cup plain yogurt
½ cup vegetable oil
½ cup honey
2 teaspoons grated lemon peel
1 to 2 tablespoons lemon juice

Heat oven to 375°. In large bowl, combine cereal, flour, baking powder and salt. In small bowl, mix egg, yogurt, oil, honey, lemon peel and juice. Add liquid mixture to flour mixture, stirring just until moistened. Batter will be lumpy. Spoon batter into 12 greased 2½-inch muffin cups. Bake 20 to 25 minutes or until golden brown. Remove from pan; cool on wire racks. *Makes 12 muffins*

Almond Crunch Muffins

⅓ cup DOLE™ Sliced Natural
    Almonds
1 can (8 ounces) DOLE® Crushed
    Pineapple
2 eggs, beaten
⅓ cup packed light brown sugar
¼ cup vegetable oil

1 cup all-purpose flour
1 cup whole wheat flour
2 teaspoons baking powder
½ teaspoon ground cinnamon
¼ teaspoon salt
1 cup chopped dried apples
½ cup DOLE™ Raisins

Generously grease 12 (2½-inch) muffin cups. Sprinkle with ¼ cup of the almonds; set aside. In small bowl, combine undrained pineapple, eggs, sugar and oil. In large bowl, combine flours, baking powder, cinnamon and salt. Pour in pineapple mixture. Stir just until blended. Fold in apples and raisins. Spoon into muffin cups. Sprinkle with remaining almonds. Bake in 400° oven 20 to 25 minutes or until wooden pick inserted in center comes out clean. Remove from pan. *Makes 12 muffins*

Dilly Cheese Muffins

2 cups all-purpose flour
1 tablespoon sugar
1 tablespoon baking powder
2 teaspoons dried dill weed
1 teaspoon onion powder
½ teaspoon salt
¼ teaspoon freshly ground black
    pepper

1 cup creamed small curd cottage
    cheese
¾ cup milk
¼ cup butter or margarine, melted
1 egg, beaten

Preheat oven to 400°. Grease or paper-line 12 (2½-inch) muffin cups. In large bowl, combine flour, sugar, baking powder, dill weed, onion powder, salt and pepper. In small bowl, combine cottage cheese, milk, butter and egg until blended. Stir into flour mixture just until moistened. Spoon into muffin cups. Bake 20 to 25 minutes or until golden and wooden pick inserted in center comes out clean. Remove from pan. *Makes 12 muffins*

Jalapeño Corn Muffins

Jalapeño peppers add zing to cornmeal muffins. These are great served with an omelet or with chili.

1½ cups stone ground cornmeal
½ cup all-purpose flour
1 tablespoon sugar
2 teaspoons baking powder
½ teaspoon baking soda

½ teaspoon salt
1 cup sour cream
2 eggs
1 to 2 teaspoons minced jalapeño
   peppers

Preheat oven to 350°. Grease 12 (2½-inch) or 36 miniature muffin cups. In large bowl, combine cornmeal, flour, sugar, baking powder, baking soda and salt. In small bowl, combine sour cream, eggs and jalapeño peppers until blended. Stir into flour mixture just until moistened. Spoon into muffin cups. Bake 20 to 25 minutes for regular-size muffins, 12 to 15 minutes for miniature muffins or until wooden pick inserted in center comes out clean. Remove from pan.

Makes 12 regular-size or 36 miniature muffins

Blue Ribbon Muffins

2 cups all-purpose flour
3 tablespoons brown sugar
1 tablespoon baking powder
½ teaspoon salt
1 egg

¼ cup butter or margarine, melted
1 cup milk
1 cup fresh blueberries
2 tablespoons granulated sugar

Preheat oven to 425°. Grease 12 (2½-inch) muffin cups. In large bowl, combine flour, brown sugar, baking powder and salt. In small bowl, combine egg, butter and milk until blended. Add to flour mixture, stirring just until moistened. Fold in blueberries. Spoon into muffin cups. Sprinkle granulated sugar over tops. Bake 20 to 25 minutes or until wooden pick inserted in center comes out clean. Remove from pan. Serve warm.

Makes 12 muffins

Favorite recipe from **United Fresh Fruit and Vegetable Association**

Tunnel of Cheese Muffins

2 cups biscuit baking mix
5 slices bacon, crisp-cooked and
   crumbled

¾ cup milk
1 egg, beaten
12 (½-inch) cubes Swiss cheese

In medium bowl, combine biscuit mix and bacon. Add milk and egg, stirring just until moistened. Spoon ½ of the batter into 12 buttered 2½-inch muffin cups. Press a cheese cube into each cup. Top with remaining batter, covering cheese completely. Bake in preheated 400° oven 25 minutes or until golden. Remove from pan. Serve hot.

Makes 12 muffins

Favorite recipe from **Wisconsin Milk Marketing Board© 1989**

Cheddar Pepper Muffins

Cheddar Pepper Muffins

These are especially light, and when eaten hot, the cheese inside the muffins is stringy.

2 cups all-purpose flour
1 tablespoon sugar
1 tablespoon baking powder
1 teaspoon coarsely cracked black pepper
½ teaspoon salt

1¼ cups milk
¼ cup vegetable oil
1 egg
1 cup (4 ounces) shredded sharp Cheddar cheese

Preheat oven to 400°. Generously grease 12 (2½-inch) muffin cups. In large bowl, combine flour, sugar, baking powder, pepper and salt. In small bowl, combine milk, oil and egg until blended. Stir into flour mixture just until moistened. Fold in ¾ cup of the cheese. Spoon into muffin cups. Sprinkle remaining cheese over tops. Bake 15 to 20 minutes or until light golden brown. Let cool in pan on wire rack 5 minutes. Remove from pan and serve warm. *Makes 12 muffins*

Treasure Bran Muffins

1¼ cups wheat bran cereal
1 cup milk
¼ cup vegetable oil
1 egg, beaten
1¼ cups all-purpose flour
½ cup sugar
1 tablespoon baking powder

½ teaspoon salt
½ cup raisins
1 (8-ounce) package PHILADELPHIA BRAND® Cream Cheese*, softened
¼ cup sugar
1 egg, beaten

In large bowl, combine cereal and milk. Let stand 2 minutes. In small bowl, combine oil and 1 egg; stir into cereal mixture. In medium bowl, combine flour, ½ cup sugar, baking powder and salt. Add to cereal mixture, stirring just until moistened. Fold in raisins. Spoon into greased and floured 2½-inch muffin cups, filling each ⅔ full.

In small bowl, combine cream cheese, ¼ cup sugar and 1 egg, mixing until well blended. Drop rounded measuring tablespoonfuls of cream cheese mixture onto batter. Bake at 375° 25 minutes. Remove from pan. *Makes 12 muffins*

*Light PHILADELPHIA BRAND® Neufchâtel Cheese may be substituted.

Cheddar Almond Muffins

Topping
- 2 tablespoons butter, melted
- 1 teaspoon Worcestershire sauce
- ½ teaspoon garlic salt
- ⅓ cup chopped blanched slivered almonds

Muffins
- 2 cups sifted all-purpose flour
- ¼ cup sugar
- 1 tablespoon baking powder
- 1 teaspoon salt
- ¾ cup (3 ounces) shredded Cheddar cheese
- 1 cup milk
- 1 egg
- 3 tablespoons butter, melted

To make topping: In bowl, blend together butter, Worcestershire sauce and garlic salt. Stir in almonds; set aside.

To make muffins: In large bowl, sift together flour, sugar, baking powder and salt. Stir in cheese. In small bowl, beat together milk and egg; stir in remaining butter. Add to dry ingredients just until moistened, about 25 stokes. Spoon into buttered muffin cups, filling ⅔ full. Sprinkle about 1 teaspoon of the almond mixture over each muffin, pressing almonds into batter slightly. Bake in preheated 400° oven 20 to 25 minutes or until golden brown. Remove from muffin cups; serve warm.

Makes 12 muffins

Variations

Parmesan Almond Muffins: Follow above directions, except substitute ½ cup grated Parmesan cheese for the Cheddar cheese.

Pineapple Muffins: Omit almond topping. Follow muffin directions, except fold in ½ cup (8½ oz. can) drained crushed pineapple.

Favorite recipe from **Wisconsin Milk Marketing Board**© **1989**

Favorite Corn Muffins

- 1 cup all-purpose flour
- ¾ cup cornmeal
- ¼ cup wheat bran cereal
- 2 teaspoons baking powder
- 1½ teaspoons salt
- ½ teaspoon baking soda
- 1 cup dairy sour cream
- 2 eggs
- ¼ cup honey
- ¼ cup butter, melted

In large bowl, combine flour, cornmeal, bran, baking powder, salt and baking soda. In medium bowl, beat sour cream, eggs, honey and butter until blended. Add to flour mixture, stirring just until moistened. Spoon batter into generously buttered 2½-inch muffin cups. Bake in preheated 425° oven 15 to 20 minutes or until wooden pick inserted in center comes out clean. Cool in pan on wire rack 5 minutes. Remove from pan. Serve warm.

Makes 12 muffins

Favorite recipe from **Wisconsin Milk Marketing Board**© **1989**

Cheesy Green Onion Muffins

Cheesy Green Onion Muffins

1 package (3 ounces) cream cheese	2 eggs, beaten
1¾ cups all-purpose flour	1¼ cups milk
4 teaspoons baking powder	⅓ cup vegetable oil
1 tablespoon sugar	½ cup chopped green onions with
1 teaspoon salt	tops
3 cups RICE CHEX® Brand Cereal, crushed to 1 cup	

Preheat oven to 400°. Grease 18 (2½-inch) muffin cups. Cut and separate cream cheese into ¼-inch cubes; set aside. In large bowl, combine flour, baking powder, sugar and salt. In medium bowl, combine cereal, eggs, milk, oil and onions. Add all at once to flour mixture, stirring just until moistened. Fold in cheese. Spoon into muffin cups. Bake 20 to 25 minutes or until wooden pick inserted in center comes out clean. Remove from pan. *Makes 18 muffins*

Calico Bell Pepper Muffins

Calico Bell Pepper Muffins

This is a rather moist batter, but results in a light and tender muffin. This is especially good with roasted or grilled chicken.

¼ cup *each* finely chopped red,
　 yellow and green bell pepper
¼ cup butter or margarine
2 cups all-purpose flour
2 tablespoons sugar

1 tablespoon baking powder
¾ teaspoon salt
½ teaspoon dried basil leaves
1 cup milk
2 eggs

Preheat oven to 400°. Grease or paper-line 12 (2½-inch) muffin cups. In small skillet, over medium-high heat, cook peppers in butter until color is bright and pepper is tender crisp about 3 minutes. Set aside.

In large bowl, combine flour, sugar, baking powder, salt and basil. In small bowl, combine milk and eggs until blended. Add milk mixture and peppers with dripping to flour mixture. Stir just until moistened. Spoon into muffin cups. Bake 15 minutes or until golden and wooden pick inserted in center comes out clean. Remove from pan.
Makes 12 muffins

Bacon Topped Chili Corn Bread Muffins

Serve these muffins with a "Tex-Mex" style meal; they would be great with a taco salad.

4 slices bacon, diced
1½ cups stone ground yellow
　 cornmeal
½ cup all-purpose flour
¼ cup instant minced onion
1 tablespoon sugar
2 teaspoons baking powder
1 teaspoon baking soda
½ teaspoon salt

1 cup buttermilk
1 can (4 ounces) chopped green
　 chilies, drained
2 eggs
3 tablespoons bacon drippings,
　 melted butter or margarine,
　 or oil
1 cup (4 ounces) ½-inch cubes
　 Monterey Jack cheese

Preheat oven to 400°. Grease 12 (2½-inch) muffin cups. In heavy skillet, over medium-high heat, cook bacon until crisp. Drain and reserve drippings. Reserve bacon bits.

In large bowl, combine cornmeal, flour, minced onion, sugar, baking powder, baking soda and salt. In small bowl, combine buttermilk, chilies, eggs and bacon drippings until blended. Stir into flour mixture just until moistened. Fold in cheese. Spoon into muffin cups. Sprinkle bacon bits over tops. Bake 15 to 20 minutes or until lightly browned. Remove from pan.
Makes 12 muffins

Pear Cheese Muffins

2 cups all-purpose flour
⅓ cup sugar
1 tablespoon baking powder
½ teaspoon salt
¼ teaspoon pumpkin pie spice
1 cup (4 ounces) shredded Colby
   cheese

2 medium pears, pared, cored, cut
   into large pieces
1 cup milk
2 large eggs
¼ cup butter, melted

In large bowl, combine flour, sugar, baking powder, salt and spice; stir in cheese. In blender or food processor, process pears, milk, eggs and butter until pears are finely chopped. Pour pear mixture into flour mixture, stirring just until moistened. Spoon into paper-lined 2½-inch muffin cups, filling ⅔ full. Bake in preheated 425° oven 20 to 25 minutes or until wooden pick inserted in center comes out clean. Serve warm.

Makes about 15 muffins

Favorite recipe from **American Dairy Association**

Peachy Drop Muffins

2 cups NABISCO® 100% Bran
1 cup skim milk
1 cup all-purpose flour
⅓ cup packed light brown sugar
2 teaspoons DAVIS® Baking
   Powder
½ teaspoon baking soda

¼ cup FLEISCHMANN'S®
   Margarine, melted
¼ cup EGG BEATERS® 99% Real
   Egg Product*
½ cup chopped canned peaches
½ cup dark seedless raisins

In medium bowl, combine bran and milk; let stand 5 minutes. In small bowl, combine flour, sugar, baking powder and baking soda; set aside. Blend margarine and Egg Beaters® into bran mixture. Stir in flour mixture just until moistened. Fold in peaches and raisins.

Drop batter by ¼ cupfuls, 2 inches apart, onto greased baking sheet or spoon batter into 12 greased 2½-inch muffin cups. Bake at 400° for 18 to 20 minutes or wooden pick inserted in center comes out clean. Serve warm.   *Makes 12 muffins*

Nutrition information per muffin
Calories 155, Dietary fiber 5 g, Cholesterol 0 mg

*Two egg whites can be substituted for the Egg Beaters.

Lemon Tea Muffins

Lemon Tea Muffins

2 cups unsifted flour	½ cup REALEMON® Lemon Juice
2 teaspoons baking powder	from Concentrate
½ teaspoon salt	¼ cup finely chopped nuts
1 cup margarine or butter, softened	2 tablespoons light brown sugar
1 cup granulated sugar	¼ teaspoon ground nutmeg
4 eggs, separated	

Preheat oven to 375°. In medium bowl, combine flour, baking powder and salt. In large bowl, beat margarine and granulated sugar until fluffy. Add egg yolks; beat until light. Gradually stir in ReaLemon® brand alternately with dry ingredients (do not overmix). In small bowl, beat egg whites until stiff but not dry. Fold ⅓ egg whites into batter; fold in remaining egg whites. Fill paper-lined or greased 2½-inch muffin cups ¾ full. In another small bowl, combine remaining ingredients; sprinkle evenly over muffins. Bake 15 to 20 minutes or until set. Cool in pan on wire rack 5 minutes. Remove from pan. Serve warm. *Makes about 18 muffins*

SNACK-TIME
M U F F I N S

Muffins make a great between-meal treat whether it's for a coffee break, after-school snack or late-night munchie. The muffins in this chapter range from sweet to hearty. There's sure to be one to please everyone. Pictured here are Crunch Top Blueberry Muffins, Pineapple Carrot Raisin Muffins and Taffy Apple Muffins. See pages 46 and 60 for recipes.

Crunch Top Blueberry Muffins

Crunch Topping (recipe follows)
2 cups all-purpose flour
⅔ cups sugar
1 tablespoon baking powder
½ teaspoon salt

½ teaspoon ground nutmeg
1½ cups blueberries*
¾ cup milk
½ cup butter or margarine, melted
2 eggs, beaten

Preheat oven to 400°. Grease or paper-line 6 (4-inch) muffin cups. Prepare Crunch Topping; set aside.

In large bowl, combine flour, sugar, baking powder, salt and nutmeg. Add 1 tablespoon of the flour mixture to the blueberries, tossing to coat. In small bowl, combine milk, butter and eggs until blended. Stir into flour mixture just until moistened. Fold in blueberries. Spoon evenly into muffin cups. Sprinkle Crunch Topping over tops. Bake 30 to 35 minutes or until wooden pick inserted in center comes out clean. Remove from pan. Cool on wire rack.   *Makes 6 giant muffins*

Crunch Topping: In medium bowl, combine ½ cup uncooked rolled oats, ½ cup all-purpose flour, ¼ cup packed brown sugar and 1 teaspoon ground cinnamon. With fork, blend in ¼ cup softened butter or margarine until mixture is crumbly.

*If you are using frozen blueberries, do not thaw. Baking time may need to be increased by up to 10 minutes.

Taffy Apple Muffins

These apple studded miniature muffins are baked, then dipped in a honey-brown sugar glaze and rolled in chopped walnuts.

2 cups all-purpose flour
½ cup granulated sugar
1 tablespoon baking powder
½ teaspoon salt
¼ teaspoon ground nutmeg
½ cup milk
¼ cup butter or margarine, melted

2 eggs
1 teaspoon vanilla
1 cup chopped apple
½ cup honey
½ cup packed dark brown sugar
¾ cup finely chopped walnuts

Preheat oven to 400°. Grease 36 miniature muffin cups. In large bowl, combine flour, granulated sugar, baking powder, salt and nutmeg. In small bowl, combine milk, butter, eggs and vanilla until blended. Stir into flour mixture just until moistened. Fold in apple. Spoon into muffin cups. Bake 10 to 12 minutes or until lightly browned and wooden pick inserted in center comes out clean. Remove from pan.

Meanwhile, in small saucepan, heat honey and brown sugar over medium-high heat to a boil; stir to dissolve sugar. Dip warm muffins into hot glaze, then into chopped nuts. Spear with popsicle sticks or wooden skewers, if desired.

Makes 36 miniature muffins

Sweet Surprise Muffins

1¾ cups unsifted flour
¼ cup sugar
2 teaspoons baking powder
1 teaspoon ground cinnamon
¾ teaspoon salt
2 eggs

¾ cup BORDEN® *or* MEADOW
   GOLD® Milk
¼ cup margarine or butter, melted
½ cup chopped nuts
¾ cup BAMA® Blackberry or
   Strawberry Preserves

Preheat oven to 400°. In small bowl, combine flour, sugar, baking powder, cinnamon and salt. In medium bowl, beat eggs; stir in milk and margarine. Add dry ingredients; stir only until moistened (batter will be slightly lumpy). Stir in nuts. Fill paper-lined 2½-inch muffin cups ⅓ full; drop 2 level teaspoons preserves into center of each. Add remaining batter to fill cups ⅔ full. Bake 20 minutes or until golden brown. Remove from pans; serve warm.   *Makes about 12 muffins*

Sweet Surprise Muffins and Fruit Blossom Muffins (see page 57)

Honey Fig Whole Wheat Muffins

Honey Fig Whole Wheat Muffins

Healthy tasting, these muffins are stuffed with figs, nuts and wheat germ.

1 cup whole wheat flour
½ cup all-purpose flour
½ cup wheat germ
2 teaspoons baking powder
1 teaspoon ground cinnamon
½ teaspoon salt
½ teaspoon ground nutmeg

½ cup milk
½ cup honey
¼ cup butter or margarine, melted
1 egg
1 cup chopped dried figs
½ cup chopped walnuts

Preheat oven to 375°. Grease or paper-line 12 (2½-inch) muffin cups. In large bowl, combine flours, wheat germ, baking powder, cinnamon, salt and nutmeg. In small bowl, combine milk, honey, butter and egg until well blended. Stir into flour mixture just until moistened. Fold in figs and nuts. Spoon into muffin cups. Bake 20 minutes or until lightly browned on edges and wooden pick inserted in center comes out clean. Remove from pan.

Makes 12 muffins

Banana Chocolate Chip Muffins

2 extra-ripe, medium DOLE™
   Bananas, peeled
2 eggs
1 cup packed brown sugar
½ cup butter or margarine, melted
1 teaspoon vanilla

2¼ cups all-purpose flour
2 teaspoons baking powder
½ teaspoon ground cinnamon
½ teaspoon salt
1 cup chocolate chips
½ cup chopped walnuts

Puree bananas in blender (1 cup). In medium bowl, beat pureed bananas, eggs, sugar, butter and vanilla until well blended. In large bowl, combine flour, baking powder, cinnamon and salt. Stir in chocolate chips and nuts. Make well in center of dry ingredients. Pour in banana mixture. Mix until just blended. Spoon into well greased 2½-inch muffin cups. Bake in 350° oven 25 to 30 minutes. Remove from pan.

Makes 12 muffins

Sour Cream Lemon Streusel Muffins

A buttery wheat germ streusel crowns these lemon-flavored muffins. They are good served plain or with butter and strawberry jam.

2 cups all-purpose flour
½ cup sugar
1 tablespoon baking powder
1 teaspoon grated lemon peel
½ teaspoon salt
1 cup chopped walnuts

½ cup sour cream
½ cup milk
½ cup butter or margarine, melted
1 egg, beaten
1 tablespoon sugar

Preheat oven to 400°. Grease or paper-line 12 (2½-inch) or 6 (4-inch) muffin cups. In large bowl, combine flour, ½ cup sugar, baking powder, lemon peel, salt and walnuts. In small bowl, combine sour cream, milk, butter and egg until blended. Stir into flour mixture just until moistened. Spoon into muffin cups. Sprinkle remaining 1 tablespoon sugar over tops. Bake 15 to 20 minutes for regular-size muffins, 20 to 25 minutes for giant-size muffins or until wooden pick inserted in center comes out clean. Remove from pan. Cool on wire rack.

Makes 12 regular-size muffins or 6 giant muffins

Banana Scotch Muffins

1 ripe, large DOLE™ Banana, peeled
1 egg, beaten
½ cup sugar
¼ cup milk
¼ cup vegetable oil
1 teaspoon vanilla

1 cup all-purpose flour
1 cup quick-cooking rolled oats
1 teaspoon baking powder
½ teaspoon baking soda
½ teaspoon salt
½ cup butterscotch chips

Puree banana in blender (⅔ cup). In medium bowl, combine pureed banana, egg, sugar, milk, oil and vanilla. In large bowl, combine flour, oats, baking powder, baking soda and salt. Stir banana mixture into dry ingredients with butterscotch chips until just blended. Spoon into well greased 2½-inch muffin cups. Bake in 400° oven 12 to 15 minutes. Remove from pan.

Makes 12 muffins

Sour Cream Lemon Streusel Muffins

Sesame Crunch Banana Muffins

A satisfying muffin with a spicy nut topping.

2 ripe, medium DOLE™ Bananas, peeled
1 cup milk
1 egg
¼ cup vegetable oil
1 teaspoon vanilla

1½ cups quick-cooking rolled oats
½ cup all-purpose flour
½ cup whole wheat flour
1 tablespoon baking powder
½ teaspoon salt
Sesame Crunch (recipe follows)

Puree bananas in blender (1 cup). In large bowl, combine pureed bananas, milk, egg, oil and vanilla; set aside. In large bowl, combine oats, flours, baking powder and salt. Stir in banana mixture just until dry ingredients are moistened (batter will be lumpy). Fill 12 greased 2½-inch muffin cups about ¾ full. Sprinkle 2 teaspoons Sesame Crunch over batter in each cup. Bake in 400° oven 20 to 25 minutes or until golden on top and wooden pick inserted in center comes out clean. Cool slightly in pan before turning out onto wire rack. Serve warm. *Makes 12 muffins*

Sesame Crunch: In small bowl, combine ¼ cup chopped nuts, 2 tablespoons *each* brown sugar and sesame seeds, 1 tablespoon whole wheat flour and ¼ teaspoon *each* ground cinnamon and nutmeg. Cut in 2 tablespoons butter or margarine until crumbly.

Sesame Crunch Banana Muffins

Blueberry Streusel Muffins

Streusel Topping (recipe follows)
⅓ cup sugar
¼ cup butter or margarine, softened
1 egg
2⅓ cups all-purpose flour

1 tablespoon plus 1 teaspoon
   baking powder
1 cup milk
1 teaspoon vanilla
1½ cups fresh blueberries

Preheat oven to 375°. Paper-line 2½-inch muffins cups. Prepare Streusel Topping; set aside.

In large bowl, cream sugar and butter until light and fluffy. Add egg, mixing well. In small bowl, combine flour and baking powder. Alternately add flour mixture and milk to the butter mixture, stirring well after each addition. Stir in vanilla. Fold in blueberries. Spoon into muffin cups. Sprinkle Streusel Topping over tops. Bake 25 to 30 minutes or until wooden pick inserted in center comes out clean. Remove from pan. *Makes 16 to 18 muffins*

Streusel Topping: In small bowl, combine ½ cup sugar, ⅓ cup all-purpose flour and ½ teaspoon ground cinnamon. Cut in ¼ cup cold butter or margarine until mixture resembles crumbs.

Favorite recipe from **United Fresh Fruit and Vegetable Association**

Bran News® Apple Muffins

2 cups BRAN NEWS® Brand Cereal
¾ cup milk
1 egg, beaten
¾ cup peeled, finely chopped apple
   (about 1 medium)
¼ cup raisins

¼ cup honey
2 tablespoons vegetable oil
1¼ cups all-purpose flour
2 teaspoons baking powder
½ teaspoon ground cinnamon

Preheat oven to 400°. Grease or paper-line 12 (2½-inch) muffin cups. In medium bowl, combine cereal, milk, egg, apple, raisins, honey and oil. Let stand 10 minutes. In large bowl, combine flour, baking powder and cinnamon. Add cereal mixture to flour mixture all at once, stirring just until moistened. Spoon into muffin cups. Bake 15 to 17 minutes or until wooden pick inserted in center comes out clean. Remove from pan. *Makes 12 muffins*

Peanut Butter Banana Muffins

1½ cups unsifted flour
1 teaspoon baking powder
1 teaspoon baking soda
½ cup BORDEN® or MEADOW GOLD® Whipping Cream
6 tablespoons margarine or butter, softened
⅓ cup LAURA SCUDDER'S® All Natural or BAMA® Peanut Butter
¼ cup packed light brown sugar
2 large, ripe bananas, mashed
½ cup CARY'S®, VERMONT MAPLE ORCHARD or MACDONALD'S Pure Maple Syrup
1 egg
1 teaspoon vanilla
¼ cup chopped peanuts

Preheat oven to 350°. In small bowl, combine flour, baking powder and baking soda. In large mixer bowl, beat cream, margarine, peanut butter and sugar until smooth. Add bananas, maple syrup, egg and vanilla; mix well. Add flour mixture; stir until moistened. Fill paper-lined 2½-inch muffin cups ¾ full; sprinkle with nuts. Bake 25 to 30 minutes or until golden brown. Remove from pans; serve warm.

Makes about 12 muffins

Spur-of-the-Moment Muffins

2 cups whole bran cereal
2 cups buttermilk
2 eggs, slightly beaten
1 can (20 ounces) DOLE® Crushed Pineapple
½ cup butter or margarine, melted
2½ cups all-purpose flour
¾ cup packed dark brown sugar
2 teaspoons salt
2 teaspoons baking soda
1 cup DOLE™ Chopped Natural Almonds, toasted

In large bowl, combine bran and buttermilk; let stand 5 minutes to soften. Stir in eggs, undrained pineapple and melted butter. In medium bowl, combine flour, brown sugar, salt, baking soda and nuts. Add to bran mixture all at once. Stir until just mixed; batter will be lumpy. Spoon into greased 2½-inch muffin cups, making only the amount you need today. Bake in 375° oven about 25 minutes. Refrigerate remaining batter, tightly covered, up to 3 weeks.

Makes about 24 muffins

Quick Cocoa-Bran Muffins

Quick Cocoa-Bran Muffins

1 package (10.75 ounces) bran and
    honey muffin mix
¼ cup HERSHEY'S Cocoa
1 egg, slightly beaten

¾ cup water
½ cup raisins
½ cup finely chopped nuts (optional)

Heat oven to 400°. Grease or paper-line 12 (2½-inch) muffin cups. In large bowl, combine muffin mix and cocoa. Stir in egg and water just until blended. Stir in raisins and nuts, if desired. Fill muffin cups ¾ full with batter. Bake 15 to 17 minutes or until wooden pick inserted in center comes out clean. Serve warm.

Makes about 12 muffins

Cherry Peanut Butter Muffins

Cherry Peanut Butter Muffins

2 cups all-purpose flour
⅓ cup sugar
2½ teaspoons baking powder
½ teaspoon salt
½ teaspoon grated orange peel
½ cup peanut butter

2 tablespoons butter or margarine
½ cup red maraschino cherries,
   chopped
⅔ cup milk
2 eggs, slightly beaten

In medium bowl, mix flour, sugar, baking powder, salt and orange peel; cut in peanut butter and butter until mixture resembles coarse crumbs. Stir in cherries. In small bowl, combine milk and eggs; stir into dry ingredients just until mixture is moistened. Spoon batter into 12 greased 3-inch muffin cups. Bake at 400° about 15 minutes or until wooden pick inserted near center comes out clean.

Makes 12 muffins

Favorite recipe from **National Cherry Foundation**

Fruit Blossom Muffins

⅔ cups BAMA® Blackberry Jam or
   Orange Marmalade
½ cup orange juice
1 egg, slightly beaten
2 cups biscuit baking mix
⅔ cup chopped pecans

¼ cup sugar
1 tablespoon flour
½ teaspoon ground cinnamon
¼ teaspoon ground nutmeg
2 to 3 teaspoons cold margarine or
   butter

Preheat oven to 400°. In medium bowl, combine jam, orange juice and egg. Add biscuit mix; stir only until moistened (batter will be slightly lumpy). Stir in nuts. Fill greased or paper-lined 2½-inch muffin cups ⅔ full. In small bowl, combine sugar, flour and spices; cut in margarine until crumbly. Sprinkle over batter. Bake 15 to 20 minutes or until golden brown. Remove from pans; serve warm.

Makes about 12 muffins

Apple Spice Muffins

1½ cups all-purpose flour
½ cup KRETSCHMER® Original
   Wheat Germ
½ cup sugar
1 tablespoon baking powder
1¼ teaspoons ground cinnamon
½ teaspoon salt (optional)

1 cup peeled, chopped apple
1 cup 2% low-fat milk
¼ cup vegetable oil
1 egg
⅓ cup chopped nuts
2 tablespoons margarine or butter,
   melted

Heat oven to 400°. Grease bottoms only or paper-line 12 (2½-inch) muffin cups. In large bowl, combine flour, wheat germ, ¼ cup of the sugar, the baking powder, ¾ teaspoon of the cinnamon and the salt. Stir in apple. In small bowl, combine milk, oil and egg. Add to flour mixture, stirring just until moistened. Fill muffin cups almost full. In small bowl, combine remaining ¼ cup sugar, ½ teaspoon cinnamon, the nuts and margarine. Sprinkle over muffins. Bake 20 to 25 minutes or until golden brown and wooden pick inserted in center comes out clean. Remove from pan.

Makes 12 muffins

Tips

To freeze muffins: Wrap securely in foil or place in freezer bag. Seal, label and freeze.

To reheat frozen muffins: Unwrap muffins. Microwave at HIGH (100%) about 30 seconds per muffin.

Nutrition information: Each serving (1 muffin)
Calories 210, Carbohydrate 26 g, Protein 5 g, Fat 10 g, Sodium 150 mg, Calcium 95 mg,
Cholesterol 25 mg, Dietary Fiber 1 g

Backpack Banana Muffins

2 extra-ripe, large DOLE™ Bananas, peeled
1 cup whole bran cereal (not flakes)
¼ cup milk
2 eggs
1 cup packed brown sugar
½ cup butter or margarine, melted
1 teaspoon vanilla
1¼ cups all-purpose flour
2 teaspoons baking powder
1 teaspoon ground cinnamon
½ teaspoon salt

Puree bananas in blender (1¼ cups). In small bowl, mix bran and milk to soften slightly. Add cereal mixture to blender along with eggs, sugar, butter and vanilla. Blend and stir until well mixed. In large bowl, combine remaining ingredients. Pour in banana mixture. Stir until just blended. Pour into greased 2½-inch muffin cups. Bake in 350° oven 25 to 30 minutes. Remove from pan.   *Makes 12 muffins*

Cinnamon Chip Muffins

2 cups all-purpose biscuit baking mix
¼ cup sugar
1 egg
⅔ cup milk
1 cup HERSHEY'S MINI CHIPS Semi-Sweet Chocolate
¼ cup finely chopped nuts (optional)
Sugar-Cinnamon Topping (recipe follows)

Heat oven to 400°. Grease or paper-line 12 (2½-inch) muffin cups. In large bowl, combine baking mix, sugar, egg and milk. Beat with spoon 30 seconds. Stir in MINI CHIPS Chocolate and nuts, if desired. Fill muffin cups ¾ full with batter. Sprinkle each with about ½ teaspoon Sugar-Cinnamon Topping. Bake 15 to 17 minutes or until very lightly browned. Serve warm.   *Makes about 12 muffins*

Sugar-Cinnamon Topping: In small bowl, combine 2 tablespoons sugar and 2 teaspoons ground cinnamon.

Cheesy Peperoni Bites

½ pound SWIFT PREMIUM® or
   MARGHERITA® Deli Sandwich
   Peperoni, unsliced
1 cup all-purpose flour
1 cup yellow cornmeal
4 teaspoons baking powder
¼ teaspoon salt

⅛ teaspoon ground red pepper
2 eggs, slightly beaten
1 cup milk
¼ cup vegetable oil
½ cup (2 ounces) shredded
   Monterey Jack cheese
¼ cup drained diced green chilies

Preheat oven to 400°. Cut five ⅛-inch-thick slices from peperoni; cut each slice into
8 wedges. Set aside. Cut remaining peperoni into ¼-inch cubes. Combine flour,
cornmeal, baking powder, salt and pepper in large mixing bowl. Combine eggs, milk
and oil in small bowl; add to flour mixture, stirring just until dry ingredients are
moistened. Fold in cheese, chilies and cubed peperoni. Spoon batter into greased
mini-muffin cups, filling each almost to top. Top each muffin with 1 wedge of
reserved peperoni, pressing halfway into batter. Bake 10 to 12 minutes or until
golden brown. Remove from pans immediately and serve warm or at room
temperature.   *Makes about 3½ dozen muffins*

Cheesy Peperoni Bites

Pineapple Carrot Raisin Muffins

Pineapple Carrot Raisin Muffins

2 cups all-purpose flour
1 cup sugar
2 teaspoons baking powder
½ teaspoon ground cinnamon
¼ teaspoon ground ginger
½ cup shredded carrots
½ cup DOLE™ Raisins

½ cup chopped walnuts
1 can (8 ounces) DOLE® Crushed
   Pineapple
2 eggs
½ cup butter or margarine, melted
1 teaspoon vanilla

In large bowl, combine flour, sugar, baking powder, cinnamon and ginger. Stir in carrots, raisins and nuts. In small bowl, combine undrained pineapple, eggs, butter and vanilla. Stir into dry ingredients until just blended. Spoon into greased 2½-inch muffin cups. Bake in 375° oven 20 to 25 minutes. Remove from pan; cool on wire rack. *Makes 12 muffins*

Cherry Blossom Muffins

1 egg
⅔ cup BAMA® Cherry or Strawberry
    Preserves
¼ cup BORDEN® *or* MEADOW
    GOLD® Milk
½ cup sugar
2 cups biscuit baking mix

⅔ cup chopped pecans
1 tablespoon flour
¾ teaspoon ground cinnamon
2 tablespoons cold margarine or
    butter
Additional chopped pecans

Preheat oven to 400°. In medium bowl, beat egg; stir in preserves, milk and *¼ cup* sugar. Add biscuit mix; stir only until moistened (batter will be slightly lumpy). Stir in *⅔ cup* nuts. Fill greased or paper-lined 2½-inch muffin cups ¾ full. In small bowl, combine remaining *¼ cup* sugar, flour and cinnamon. Cut in margarine until crumbly; sprinkle over batter. Top with additional nuts. Bake 15 to 20 minutes or until golden brown. Remove from pans; serve warm. *Makes about 12 muffins*

Apple-Walnut Muffins

2 cups all-purpose flour
⅔ cup sugar
2¼ teaspoons baking powder
¾ teaspoon salt
¼ teaspoon ground cinnamon
1 egg

⅔ cup milk
3 tablespoons vegetable oil
1 teaspoon grated lemon peel
¾ teaspoon vanilla
1 cup chopped DIAMOND® Walnuts
¾ cup coarsely grated pared apple

In medium bowl, sift flour with sugar, baking powder, salt and cinnamon. In small bowl, beat egg; add milk, oil, lemon peel and vanilla. Stir into dry ingredients, mixing just until flour is moistened. Fold in walnuts and apple. Spoon batter into 12 greased 2½-inch muffin cups. Bake in preheated 400° oven 20 to 25 minutes or until golden brown and wooden pick inserted in center comes out clean.

Makes 12 muffins

MICROWAVE
M U F F I N S

You can cook 12 warm and delicious muffins in less than 10 minutes in a microwave oven. For best results line the microwavable muffin pan with double paper baking cups, check doneness with wooden pick before adding cooking time and let the muffins stand a few minutes before eating. Pictured here are Chocolate Chip Bran Muffins and Molasses Whole Wheat Muffins. See page 64 for recipes.

Molasses Whole Wheat Muffins

1 cup whole wheat flour
2 tablespoons all-purpose flour
2 tablespoons packed brown sugar
1 teaspoon fennel or anise seed
1 teaspoon baking powder
½ teaspoon baking soda

⅓ cup buttermilk
¼ cup dark molasses
¼ cup vegetable oil
1 egg, beaten
¼ cup raisins

Microwave: In large bowl, combine flours, brown sugar, fennel seed, baking powder and baking soda. In small bowl, combine buttermilk, molasses, oil and egg until blended. Stir into flour mixture just until moistened. Fold in raisins.

Line 6 microwavable muffin-pan cups with double paper liners. Spoon batter into each cup, filling ½ full. Microwave at HIGH (100%) 2½ to 4½ minutes or until wooden pick inserted in center comes out clean. Rotate dish ½ turn halfway through cooking. Let stand 5 minutes. Remove from pan. Repeat procedure with remaining batter. *Makes about 12 muffins*

Chocolate Chip Bran Muffins

1½ cups wheat bran flakes cereal
½ cup boiling water
1 cup buttermilk or sour milk*
¼ cup vegetable oil
1 egg, slightly beaten
1¼ cups all-purpose flour
½ cup sugar

1 teaspoon baking soda
¼ teaspoon salt
½ cup HERSHEY'S MINI CHIPS
   Semi-Sweet Chocolate
¼ cup finely chopped dried apricots
¾ cup wheat bran flakes cereal

Microwave: In medium bowl, combine 1½ cups cereal and boiling water; blend well. Cool. Add buttermilk, oil and egg; blend well. In another medium bowl, combine flour, sugar, baking soda and salt. Stir in cereal mixture, MINI CHIPS Chocolate and apricots just until dry ingredients are moistened.

Place 6 paper muffin cups (2½ inches in diameter) in microwavable muffin pan or 6-ounce microwavable custard cups. Fill each cup ½ full with batter. Sprinkle 2 teaspoons cereal on each muffin. Microwave at HIGH (100%) 2½ to 3½ minutes, turning ¼ turn every minute or until wooden pick inserted in center comes out clean. (Tops may still appear moist.) Let stand several minutes. (Moist spots will disappear upon standing.) Repeat cooking procedure with remaining batter. Serve warm. *Makes about 18 muffins*

*To sour milk: Use 1 tablespoon vinegar plus milk to equal 1 cup. Stir; let stand 5 minutes.

Oat Bran Muffins

Oat Bran Muffins

1½ cups NABISCO WHOLESOME 'N
HEARTY OAT BRAN™ Hot
Cereal
¾ cup all-purpose flour
1 tablespoon baking powder
½ cup skim milk

½ cup honey
¼ cup EGG BEATERS® 99% Real
Egg Product*
¼ cup FLEISCHMANN'S®
Margarine, melted and cooled

Microwave: In large bowl, combine oat bran, flour and baking powder; stir in milk, honey, Egg Beaters® and margarine just until blended.

Fill 6 paper-lined microwavable muffin-pan cups ½ full. Microwave at HIGH (100%) 2 to 2½ minutes or until wooden pick inserted in center comes out clean. Remove from pan. Serve warm. Repeat procedure with remaining batter.

Makes about 12 muffins

Conventional: Prepare batter as directed. Spoon into 12 paper-lined or greased 2½-inch muffin cups. Bake at 400° 15 to 18 minutes or until wooden pick inserted in center comes out clean. Remove from pan. Serve warm.   *Makes 12 muffins*

*Two egg whites can be substituted.

Nutrition information per muffin:
Calories 146, Sodium 127 mg, Cholesterol 0 mg, Total Fat 4 g, Saturated Fat 1 g, Dietary Fiber 2 g

Variations

Apple Walnut: Fold ½ cup *each* chopped apple and chopped walnuts into prepared batter.

Strawberry Almond: Fold ½ cup *each* chopped strawberries and chopped almonds into prepared batter.

Cinnamon Raisin: Fold 1 cup raisins and 1 teaspoon ground cinnamon into prepared batter.

Cinnamon Spiced Muffins

Cinnamon Spiced Muffins

1½ cups all-purpose flour
½ cup sugar
2 teaspoons baking powder
½ teaspoon salt
½ teaspoon ground nutmeg
½ teaspoon ground coriander
½ teaspoon ground allspice

½ cup milk
⅓ cup butter or margarine, melted
1 egg
¼ cup sugar
1 teaspoon ground cinnamon
¼ cup butter or margarine, melted

Microwave: In large bowl, combine flour, ½ cup sugar, baking powder, salt, nutmeg, coriander and allspice. In small bowl, combine milk, butter and egg. Stir into flour mixture just until moistened.

Line 6 microwavable muffin-pan cups with double paper liners. Spoon batter into each cup, filling ½ full. Microwave at HIGH (100%) 2½ to 4½ minutes or until wooden pick inserted in center comes out clean. Rotate dish ½ turn halfway through cooking. Let stand 5 minutes. Remove from pan. Repeat procedure with remaining batter.

Meanwhile, combine remaining ¼ cup sugar and cinnamon in a shallow dish. Roll warm muffins in remaining ¼ cup melted butter, then sugar-cinnamon mixture. Serve warm.

Makes about 12 muffins

Conventional: Preheat oven to 400°. Grease 36 miniature muffin cups. Prepare batter as directed. Spoon into muffin cups. Bake 10 to 13 minutes or until edges are lightly browned and wooden pick inserted in center comes out clean. Remove from pan.

Meanwhile, combine remaining ¼ cup sugar and cinnamon in a shallow dish. Roll warm muffins in remaining ¼ cup melted butter, then sugar-cinnamon mixture. Serve warm.

Makes 36 miniature muffins

Bayou Yam Muffins

1 cup all-purpose flour
1 cup yellow cornmeal
¼ cup sugar
1 tablespoon baking powder
1¼ teaspoons ground cinnamon
½ teaspoon salt
2 eggs

½ cup cold strong coffee
¼ cup butter or margarine, melted
½ teaspoon TABASCO® Pepper
    Sauce
1 cup mashed yams or sweet
    potatoes

Microwave: In large bowl, combine flour, cornmeal, sugar, baking powder, cinnamon and salt. Make well in center. In medium bowl, beat eggs; stir in coffee, butter, Tabasco® sauce and yams. Add yam mixture to flour mixture, stirring just until moistened.

Place 6 paper muffin cups in microwavable muffin pan or 6-ounce microwavable custard cups. Spoon about ⅓ cup batter into each cup. Microwave at HIGH (100%) 4 to 5½ minutes or until wooden pick inserted in center comes out clean. Rotate muffin pan ½ turn or rearrange custard cups once halfway through cooking. Let stand 5 minutes; remove from pan. Repeat procedure with remaining batter. Serve warm or at room temperature. *Makes about 12 muffins*

Conventional: Preheat oven to 425°. Grease 12 (3-inch) muffin cups. Prepare batter as directed. Spoon into muffin cups. Bake 20 to 25 minutes or until wooden pick inserted in center comes out clean. Cool in pan on wire rack 5 minutes. Remove from pan. Serve warm or at room temperature. *Makes 12 muffins*

Banana Corn Muffins

1 cup all-purpose flour
¾ cup QUAKER® *or* AUNT
    JEMIMA® Enriched Corn Meal
¼ cup sugar
1 tablespoon baking powder
½ teaspoon salt

¾ cup mashed ripe banana
½ cup milk
½ cup vegetable oil
1 egg, beaten

Microwave: In medium bowl, combine flour, corn meal, sugar, baking powder and salt. In small bowl, combine banana, milk, oil and egg. Add to flour mixture, stirring just until moistened.

Line 6 microwavable muffin-pan cups with double paper baking cups. Fill muffin cups ⅔ full. Microwave at HIGH (100%) about 1½ minutes or until wooden pick inserted in center comes out clean. Rotate dish ¼ turn after 1 minute of cooking. Remove from pan. Repeat procedure with remaining batter. Serve warm. *Makes about 15 muffins*

Conventional: Decrease vegetable oil to ⅓ cup. Heat oven to 425°. Grease or paper-line 12 (2½-inch) muffin cups. Prepare batter as directed, using only ⅓ cup vegetable oil. Fill muffin cups ¾ full. Bake 15 to 18 minutes or until golden brown or wooden pick inserted in center comes out clean. Remove from pan. *Makes 12 muffins*

Bayou Yam Muffins

Top: Chocolate Chip Bran Muffins (see page 64) Bottom: Cocoa Applesauce Muffins

Cocoa Applesauce Muffins

Crunch Topping (recipe follows)
¼ cup HERSHEY'S Cocoa
¼ cup vegetable oil
¾ cup applesauce
1 egg, beaten
1¼ cups all-purpose flour

¾ cup sugar
¾ teaspoon baking soda
¼ teaspoon salt
¼ teaspoon ground cinnamon
½ cup chopped nuts

Microwave: Prepare Crunch Topping; set aside. In small bowl, combine cocoa and oil; stir until smooth. Add applesauce and egg; blend well. In medium bowl, combine flour, sugar, baking soda, salt and cinnamon. Stir in applesauce mixture just until moistened. Fold in nuts.

Place 6 paper muffin cups (2½ inches in diameter) in microwavable muffin pan or 6-ounce microwavable custard cups. Fill each cup ½ full with batter. Sprinkle about 2 teaspoons Crunch Topping on each muffin. Microwave at HIGH (100%) 2½ to 3½ minutes, turning ¼ turn every minute or until wooden pick inserted in center comes out clean. (Tops may still appear moist.) Let stand several minutes. (Moist spots will disappear upon standing.) Repeat procedure with remaining batter. Serve warm.

Makes about 12 muffins

Crunch Topping: In small microwavable bowl, microwave 1 tablespoon butter or margarine at HIGH (100%) 15 seconds or until melted. Add 2 tablespoons HERSHEY'S Cocoa; blend until smooth. Stir in ¼ cup packed light brown sugar, ¼ cup chopped nuts, 2 tablespoons all-purpose flour and ¼ teaspoon ground cinnamon.

Louisiana Corn Muffins

1 cup all-purpose flour
1 cup yellow cornmeal
2 tablespoons sugar
2½ teaspoons baking powder
½ teaspoon salt
1 cup milk
½ cup vegetable oil

2 eggs, slightly beaten
½ teaspoon TABASCO® Pepper
Sauce
1 can (8¾ ounces) whole kernel
corn, drained or 1 cup fresh or
thawed frozen corn kernels

Microwave: In large bowl, combine flour, cornmeal, sugar, baking powder and salt. Make well in center. In medium bowl, combine milk, oil, eggs and Tabasco® sauce. Add milk mixture to flour mixture, stirring just until moistened. Fold in corn.

Place 6 paper muffin cups in microwavable muffin pan or 6-ounce microwavable custard cups. Spoon about ⅓ cup batter into each cup. Microwave at HIGH (100%) 4 to 5½ minutes or until wooden pick inserted in center comes out clean. Rotate muffin pan ½ turn or rearrange custard cups once halfway through cooking. Let stand 5 minutes; remove from pan. Repeat procedure with remaining batter. Serve warm. *Makes about 12 muffins*

Conventional: Preheat oven to 400°. Grease 12 (3-inch) muffin cups. Prepare batter as directed. Spoon into muffin cups. Bake 15 to 20 minutes or until wooden pick inserted in center comes out clean. Cool in pan on wire rack 5 minutes. Remove from pan. Serve warm. *Makes 12 muffins*

Carrot Bran Muffins

2 cups finely shredded carrots
1 cup 40% wheat bran flakes
¾ cup skim milk
2 tablespoons vegetable oil
1 tablespoon lemon juice
1 egg, slightly beaten

1 cup whole wheat flour
2 tablespoons packed brown sugar
1 teaspoon baking powder
½ teaspoon baking soda
½ teaspoon pumpkin pie spice
¼ teaspoon salt

Microwave: In large bowl, combine carrots, bran and milk. Let stand 5 minutes. Stir in oil, lemon juice and egg. In medium bowl, combine flour, sugar, baking powder, baking soda, spice and salt. Stir into bran mixture just until moistened. Batter will be lumpy.

Line 6 microwavable muffin-pan cups with double paper liners. Spoon batter into each cup, filling ½ full. Microwave at HIGH (100%) 2 to 4½ minutes or until top springs back when touched. Rotate dish ½ turn halfway through cooking. Let stand 5 minutes. Remove from pan. Repeat procedure with remaining batter. *Makes about 12 muffins*

Double Oat Muffins

The combination of oats and oat bran create a healthful grain muffin perfect for breakfast or as a snack.

2 cups QUAKER OAT BRAN™ Hot Cereal, uncooked
⅓ cup packed brown sugar
¼ cup all-purpose flour
2 teaspoons baking powder
¼ teaspoon salt (optional)
¼ teaspoon ground nutmeg (optional)

1 cup skim milk
2 egg whites, slightly beaten
3 tablespoons vegetable oil
1½ teaspoons vanilla
¼ cup QUAKER® OATS (quick or old fashioned, uncooked)
1 tablespoon packed brown sugar

Microwave: In large bowl, combine oat bran, ⅓ cup brown sugar, flour, baking powder, salt and nutmeg. In small bowl, combine milk, egg whites, oil and vanilla. Pour into oat bran mixture, mixing just until moistened.

Line 6 microwavable muffin-pan cups with double paper baking cups. Fill muffin cups almost full. In small bowl, combine oats and remaining 1 tablespoon brown sugar. Sprinkle evenly over batter. Microwave at HIGH (100%) 2½ to 3 minutes or until wooden pick inserted in center comes out clean. Remove from pan. Let stand 5 minutes before serving. Repeat procedure with remaining batter.

Makes 12 muffins

Conventional: Heat oven to 400°. Line 12 (2½-inch) muffin cups with paper baking cups. Prepare batter as directed. Fill muffin cups almost full. In small bowl, combine oats and remaining 1 tablespoon brown sugar. Sprinkle evenly over batter. Bake 20 to 22 minutes or until golden brown.

Makes 12 muffins

Tips

To freeze muffins: Wrap securely in foil or place in freezer bag. Seal, label and freeze.

To reheat frozen muffins: Unwrap muffins. Microwave at HIGH (100%) about 30 seconds per muffin.

Nutrition information: Each serving (1 muffin)
Calories 140, Protein 5 g, Carbohydrate 19 g, Fat 5 g (polyunsaturated 2 g, monounsaturated 1 g, saturated 0 g), Oat Bran 16 g, Dietary Fiber 2 g, Sodium 90 mg, Cholesterol 0 mg
Percentage of calories from fat: 31%, Diabetic exchanges: 1 Starch/Bread; 1 Fat; ½ Fruit

Double Oat Muffins

Chili Corn Muffins

Chili Corn Muffins

You can bake almost any muffin batter in the microwave oven. Because the batter rises higher during baking, be sure to fill muffin cups only ½ full.

½ cup all-purpose flour
½ cup stone ground cornmeal
1 tablespoon sugar
1 teaspoon baking powder
½ teaspoon baking soda
½ teaspoon salt
½ teaspoon chili powder

½ cup frozen or fresh whole kernel corn
¼ cup chopped green bell pepper
⅓ cup buttermilk
¼ cup vegetable oil
1 egg, beaten

Microwave: In large bowl, combine flour, cornmeal, sugar, baking powder, baking soda, salt and chili powder. Stir in corn and pepper. In small bowl, combine buttermilk, oil and egg until blended. Stir into flour mixture just until moistened.

Line 6 microwavable muffin-pan cups with double paper liners. Spoon batter into each cup, filling ½ full. Microwave at HIGH (100%) 2½ to 4½ minutes or until tops appear dry. Rotate dish ½ turn halfway through cooking. Let stand 5 minutes. Remove from pan. Repeat procedure with remaining batter.

Makes about 12 muffins

Carrot Wheat Germ Muffins

Topping (recipe follows)
1 cup all-purpose flour
¼ cup wheat germ
⅔ cup sugar
½ teaspoon baking powder
½ teaspoon baking soda
½ teaspoon ground cinnamon

⅛ teaspoon salt
1 cup shredded carrots
½ cup vegetable oil
¼ cup buttermilk
2 eggs
½ cup chopped walnuts or pecans

Microwave: Prepare Topping; set aside. In large bowl, combine flour, wheat germ, sugar, baking powder, baking soda, cinnamon, salt and carrots. In small bowl, combine oil, buttermilk and eggs. Add to flour mixture, stirring just until moistened. Fold in nuts.

Line 6 microwavable muffin-pan cups with double paper liners. Spoon batter into each cup, filling ½ full. Sprinkle Topping over batter. Microwave at HIGH (100%) 2½ to 4½ minutes or until wooden pick inserted in center comes out clean. Rotate dish ½ turn halfway through cooking. Let stand 5 minutes. Remove from pan. Repeat procedure. For last 3 muffins, line 3 muffin cups with double paper liners. Microwave at HIGH 1½ to 2 minutes. Let stand 5 minutes. Remove from pan.

Makes about 15 muffins

Topping: In small bowl, combine 1 tablespoon wheat germ, 2 teaspoons sugar and 1 teaspoon ground cinnamon.

Honey Muffins

1 can (8 ounces) DOLE® Crushed Pineapple
1½ cups wheat bran cereal (not flakes)
⅔ cup buttermilk
1 egg, slightly beaten
⅓ cup chopped pecans or walnuts
3 tablespoons vegetable oil
½ cup honey
⅔ cup whole wheat flour
½ teaspoon baking soda
⅛ teaspoon salt

Microwave: In large bowl, combine undrained pineapple, cereal and buttermilk. Let stand 10 minutes until cereal has absorbed the liquid. Stir in egg, nuts, oil and ¼ cup of the honey. In small bowl, combine flour, soda and salt. Stir into bran mixture until just moistened.

Line 6 microwavable muffin-pan cups or 6-ounce microwavable custard cups with double thickness paper baking cups. (Outer cup will absorb moisture so inner cup sticks to cooked muffin.) Spoon batter into cups, filling to the top. Microwave at HIGH (100%) 3½ to 4 minutes, rotating pan ½ turn after 1½ minutes. Muffins are done when they look dry and set on top.

Immediately upon removing from oven, spoon 1 teaspoon of the honey over each muffin. Remove to cooling rack after honey has been absorbed. Repeat procedure with remaining batter. Serve warm. *Makes 12 muffins*

Note: Muffins may be frozen and reheated.

Coffee Cake Muffins

Topping (recipe follows)
1½ cups all-purpose flour
½ cup granulated sugar
2 teaspoons baking powder
½ teaspoon salt
½ cup butter or margarine, melted
1 egg
⅓ cup milk
Icing (recipe follows)

Microwave: Prepare Topping; set aside. In large bowl, combine flour, granulated sugar, baking powder and salt. Pour in butter; add egg and milk. Stir until ingredients are blended. (Batter will be soft.)

Line 6 microwavable muffin-pan cups with double paper liners. Spoon 2 tablespoons of the batter into each cup. Sprinkle ¼ of the Topping over batter. Spoon batter over Topping, filling cups about ½ full. Sprinkle ¼ of the Topping over batter, pressing into the batter. Microwave at HIGH (100%) 2½ to 4½ minutes or until wooden pick inserted in center comes out clean. Rotate dish ½ turn halfway through cooking. Let stand 5 minutes. Remove from pan. Repeat procedure. Prepare Icing and drizzle over warm muffins. *Makes 12 muffins*

Topping: In small bowl, combine ¼ cup packed brown sugar, ¼ cup chopped walnuts, 3 tablespoons all-purpose flour and 1 teaspoon ground cinnamon. Add 1 tablespoon melted butter or margarine, stirring until mixture resembles moist crumbs.

Icing: In small bowl, combine ½ cup powdered sugar, 1 tablespoon milk and 1 teaspoon vanilla, stirring until smooth.

Honey Muffins

Raisin Orange Muffins

Raisin Orange Muffins

1 cup whole wheat flour
½ cup uncooked rolled oats
¼ cup sugar
2 teaspoons baking powder
¼ teaspoon salt
¼ teaspoon ground allspice

⅔ cup skim milk
2 eggs, slightly beaten
2 tablespoons vegetable oil
1 teaspoon grated orange peel
¼ cup raisins

Microwave: In large bowl, combine flour, oats, sugar, baking powder, salt and allspice. Make well in center. In small bowl, combine milk, eggs, oil and orange peel. Pour into flour mixture, stirring just until moistened. Batter will be lumpy. Fold in raisins.

Line 6 microwavable muffin-pan cups with double paper liners. Spoon batter into each cup, filling ½ full. Microwave at HIGH (100%) 2 to 4½ minutes or until top springs back when touched. Rotate dish ½ turn halfway through cooking. Let stand 5 minutes. Remove from pan. Repeat procedure with remaining batter.

Makes 12 muffins

Refrigerator Applesauce Wheat Muffins

Mix up this batter and refrigerate in a tightly covered plastic bowl. If you cook for one, you can scoop out batter for one muffin at a time. Bake in the microwave oven for 30 to 50 seconds.

¾ cup all-purpose flour
½ cup whole wheat flour
1 cup uncooked quick-cooking
   rolled oats
½ cup packed brown sugar
1 teaspoon baking powder
½ teaspoon baking soda

½ teaspoon ground cinnamon
¼ teaspoon salt
¾ cup buttermilk
¼ cup applesauce
¼ cup vegetable oil
1 egg, beaten
¼ cup raisins

Microwave: In large bowl, combine flours, oats, brown sugar, baking powder, baking soda, cinnamon and salt. In small bowl, combine buttermilk, applesauce, oil and egg until blended. Stir into flour mixture just until moistened. Fold in raisins. Cover and refrigerate overnight or up to 1 week.

Line 6 microwavable muffin-pan cups with double paper liners. Spoon batter into each cup, filling ½ full. Microwave at HIGH (100%) 3 to 3½ minutes or until wooden pick inserted in center comes out clean. Rotate dish ½ turn halfway through cooking. Let stand 5 minutes. Remove from pan. Repeat procedure. For last 3 muffins, line 3 muffin cups with double paper liners. Microwave at HIGH 1½ to 2 minutes. Let stand 5 minutes. Remove from pan. *Makes about 15 muffins*

Conventional: Preheat oven to 400°. Grease or paper-line 12 (2½-inch) muffin cups. Prepare batter as directed. Spoon batter into cups. Bake 18 to 20 minutes or until wooden pick inserted in center comes out clean. Remove from pan.

Makes 12 muffins

DESSERT
MUFFINS

These individual treats are a great way to complete a meal.
A compact dessert—they can be packed for
picnics or used as a delicious ending for family meals.
The muffins in this chapter will satisfy your sweet tooth.
Pictured here are Streusel Raspberry Muffins.
See page 82 for recipe.

Streusel Raspberry Muffins

The juicy tartness of raspberries is balanced by the topping of caramelized,
crunchy pecan streusel.

Pecan Streusel Topping (recipe
    follows)
1½ cups all-purpose flour
½ cup sugar
2 teaspoons baking powder

½ cup milk
½ cup butter or margarine, melted
1 egg, beaten
1 cup fresh or individually frozen,
    whole unsugared raspberries

Preheat oven to 375°. Grease or paper-line 12 (2½-inch) muffin cups. Prepare Pecan Streusel Topping; set aside.

In large bowl, combine flour, sugar and baking powder. In small bowl, combine milk, butter and egg until blended. Stir into flour mixture just until moistened. Spoon ½ of the batter into muffin cups. Divide raspberries among cups, then top with remaining batter. Sprinkle Pecan Streusel Topping over tops. Bake 25 to 30 minutes or until golden and wooden pick inserted in center comes out clean. Remove from pan. *Makes 12 muffins*

Pecan Streusel Topping: In small bowl, combine ¼ cup *each* chopped pecans, packed brown sugar and all-purpose flour. Stir in 2 tablespoons melted butter or margarine until mixture resembles moist crumbs.

Chocolate Chip Fruit Muffins

1 package (15 ounces) banana
    quick bread mix
2 eggs, slightly beaten
1 cup milk
¼ cup vegetable oil

1 cup HERSHEY'S Semi-Sweet
    Chocolate Chips, MINI CHIPS
    or Milk Chocolate Chips
½ cup dried fruit bits

Heat oven to 400°. Grease or paper-line 18 (2½-inch) muffin cups. In large bowl, combine bread mix, eggs, milk and oil. Beat with spoon 30 seconds. Stir in chocolate chips and fruit bits. Fill muffin cups ¾ full with batter. Bake 18 to 20 minutes or until lightly browned. Serve warm. *Makes about 18 muffins*

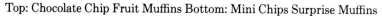

Mini Chips Surprise Muffins

1 package (16.1 ounces) nut quick
   bread mix
1 egg
1 cup milk

¼ cup vegetable oil
1 cup HERSHEY'S MINI CHIPS
   Semi-Sweet Chocolate
⅓ cup fruit preserves, any flavor

Heat oven to 400°. Grease or paper-line 18 muffin cups (2½ inches in diameter). In large bowl, combine bread mix, egg, milk and oil. Beat with spoon 1 minute. Fold in MINI CHIPS Chocolate. Spoon into muffin cups, filling ¼ full. Spoon ½ teaspoon preserves into center of batter. Fill muffin cups ¾ full with batter. Bake 20 to 22 minutes or until lightly browned. Remove from pan. Serve warm.

Makes about 18 muffins

Top: Chocolate Chip Fruit Muffins Bottom: Mini Chips Surprise Muffins

Tropical Treat Muffins

Tropical Treat Muffins

Chewy and sweet, dried papaya chunks, chopped banana chips, macadamia nuts and coconut give these muffins an exotic but healthy character.

2 cups all-purpose flour
⅓ cup sugar
1 tablespoon baking powder
1 teaspoon grated lemon peel
½ teaspoon salt
¾ cup (4 ounces) dried papaya, finely diced
½ cup coarsely chopped banana chips

½ cup chopped macadamia nuts
¼ cup flaked coconut
½ cup milk
½ cup butter or margarine, melted
¼ cup sour cream
1 egg, beaten
1 tablespoon sugar

Preheat oven to 400°. Grease or paper-line 12 (2½-inch) or 6 (4-inch) muffins cups. In large bowl, combine flour, ⅓ cup sugar, baking powder, lemon peel and salt. In small bowl, combine papaya, banana chips, nuts and coconut. Stir in 1 tablespoon of the flour mixture until well coated. In another small bowl, combine milk, butter, sour cream and egg until blended. Stir into flour mixture just until moistened. Fold in fruit mixture. Spoon into muffin cups. Sprinkle remaining 1 tablespoon sugar over tops. Bake 15 to 20 minutes for regular-size muffins, 25 to 30 minutes for giant muffins or until wooden pick inserted in center comes out clean. Remove from pan. Cool on wire rack. *Makes 12 regular-size or 6 giant muffins*

Apple Date Nut Muffins

1½ cups all-purpose flour
⅔ cup packed brown sugar
½ cup uncooked rolled oats
1 tablespoon baking powder
1 teaspoon ground cinnamon
½ teaspoon salt
⅛ teaspoon ground nutmeg
⅛ teaspoon ground ginger

Dash ground cloves
1 cup coarsely chopped pared apples
½ cup chopped walnuts
½ cup chopped pitted dates
½ cup butter or margarine, melted
¼ cup milk
2 eggs

Preheat oven to 400°. Grease well or paper-line 12 (2½-inch) muffin cups. In large bowl, combine flour, brown sugar, oats, baking powder, cinnamon, salt, nutmeg, ginger and cloves. Mix in apples, nuts and dates. In small bowl, combine butter, milk and eggs until blended. Pour into flour mixture, stirring just until moistened. Spoon into muffin cups. Bake 20 to 25 minutes or until wooden pick inserted in center comes out clean. Remove from pan. *Makes 12 muffins*

Lemon Glazed Zucchini Muffins

2 cups all-purpose flour
⅔ cups granulated sugar
1 tablespoon baking powder
1 teaspoon salt
½ teaspoon ground nutmeg
2 teaspoons grated lemon peel
¾ cup chopped walnuts, pecans or hazelnuts
½ cup dried fruit bits or golden raisins
½ cup milk
⅓ cup vegetable oil
2 eggs
1 cup zucchini, shredded, packed into cup, not drained
½ cup powdered sugar
2 to 3 teaspoons fresh lemon juice

Preheat oven to 400°. Grease well or paper-line 12 (2½-inch) muffin cups. In large bowl, combine flour, granulated sugar, baking powder, salt, nutmeg and lemon peel. Stir in nuts and fruit. In small bowl, combine milk, oil and eggs until blended. Pour into flour mixture; add zucchini, stirring just until moistened. Spoon into muffin cups. Bake 20 to 25 minutes or until wooden pick inserted in center comes out clean. Remove from pan. Meanwhile, in small bowl, combine powdered sugar and lemon juice until smooth. Drizzle over warm muffins. *Makes 12 muffins*

Pecan Peach Muffins

Topping (recipe follows)
1½ cups all-purpose flour
½ cup granulated sugar
2 teaspoons baking powder
1 teaspoon ground cinnamon
¼ teaspoon salt
½ cup butter or margarine, melted
¼ cup milk
1 egg
2 medium peaches, peeled, diced (about 1 cup)

Preheat oven to 400°. Paper-line 12 (2½-inch) muffin cups. Prepare Topping; set aside.

In large bowl, combine flour, granulated sugar, baking powder, cinnamon and salt. In small bowl, combine butter, milk and egg until blended. Pour into flour mixture, stirring just until moistened. Fold in peaches. Spoon into muffin cups. Sprinkle Topping over batter. Bake 20 to 25 minutes or until wooden pick inserted in center comes out clean. Remove from pan. *Makes 12 muffins*

Topping: In small bowl, combine ½ cup chopped pecans, ⅓ cup packed brown sugar, ¼ cup all-purpose flour and 1 teaspoon ground cinnamon. Add 2 tablespoons melted butter or margarine, stirring until mixture is crumbly.

Two Tone Muffins

Two Tone Muffins

2 cups all-purpose flour	¾ cup orange juice
½ cup sugar	⅓ cup almond oil or vegetable oil
1 tablespoon baking powder	1 egg, beaten
1 teaspoon salt	¼ cup cocoa powder
¾ cup roasted diced almonds	1 teaspoon grated orange peel

Preheat oven to 400°. Paper-line 12 (2½-inch) muffin cups. In large bowl, combine flour, sugar, baking powder and salt. Stir in almonds, reserving some for garnish. In small bowl, combine orange juice, oil and egg. Stir into flour mixture just until moistened. Transfer ½ of the batter into another small bowl; stir in cocoa and set aside. Stir orange peel into remaining batter. Carefully spoon orange batter into one side of each cup. Fill other side with cocoa batter. Sprinkle reserved almonds over tops. Bake 20 minutes or until wooden pick inserted in center comes out clean. Remove from pan. Serve warm. *Makes 12 muffins*

Favorite recipe from **Almond Board of California**

Chocolate Spice Surprise Muffins

⅓ cup packed light brown sugar
¼ cup margarine or butter, softened
1 egg
1 cup BORDEN® *or* MEADOW
   GOLD® Milk
2 cups biscuit baking mix
⅓ cup unsweetened cocoa

1 (9-ounce) package NONE SUCH®
   Condensed Mincemeat,
   crumbled
18 solid milk chocolate candy drops
½ cup confectioners' sugar
1 tablespoon water

Preheat oven to 375°. In large bowl, beat brown sugar and margarine until fluffy. Add egg and milk; mix well. Stir in biscuit mix, cocoa and mincemeat until moistened. Fill greased or paper-lined 2½-inch muffin cups ¾ full. Top with candy drop; press into batter. Bake 15 to 20 minutes. Cool in pan on wire rack 5 minutes. Remove from pan. Meanwhile, in small bowl, mix confectioners' sugar and water; drizzle over warm muffins. *Makes about 18 muffins*

Chocolate Spice Surprise Muffins

Walnut Streusel Muffins

3 cups all-purpose flour
1½ cups packed brown sugar
¾ cup butter or margarine
1 cup chopped DIAMOND® Walnuts
2 teaspoons baking powder
1 teaspoon ground nutmeg

1 teaspoon ground ginger
½ teaspoon baking soda
½ teaspoon salt
1 cup buttermilk or sour milk*
2 eggs, beaten

In medium bowl, combine 2 cups of the flour and the sugar; cut in butter to form fine crumbs. In small bowl, combine ¾ cup of the crumbs and ¼ cup of the walnuts; set aside. Into remaining crumb mixture, stir in remaining 1 cup flour, the baking powder, spices, baking soda, salt and remaining ¾ cup walnuts. In another small bowl, combine buttermilk and eggs; stir into dry ingredients just to moisten. Spoon into 18 greased or paper-lined 2¾-inch muffin cups, filling about ⅔ full. Top each with a generous spoonful of reserved crumb-nut mixture. Bake in preheated 350° oven 20 to 25 minutes or until wooden pick inserted in center comes out clean. Cool in pans on wire rack 10 minutes. Loosen and remove from pans. Serve warm.

Makes 18 muffins

*To sour milk: Use 1 tablespoon vinegar plus milk to equal 1 cup. Stir; let stand 5 minutes.

Cranberry Muffins and Creamy Orange Spread

2 cups all-purpose flour
7 tablespoons sugar
2 teaspoons baking powder
½ teaspoon salt
¾ cup milk
½ cup PARKAY® Margarine, melted
1 egg, beaten

¾ cup coarsely chopped cranberries
1 (8-ounce) package
PHILADELPHIA BRAND®
Cream Cheese*, softened
1 tablespoon orange juice
1 teaspoon grated orange peel

In large bowl, combine flour, 4 tablespoons sugar, baking powder and salt; mix well. In medium bowl, combine milk, margarine and egg. Pour into flour mixture, mixing just until moistened. In small bowl, combine 2 tablespoons sugar and cranberries; fold into batter. Spoon into greased 2½-inch muffin cups, filling each ⅔ full. Bake at 400° 20 to 25 minutes or until golden brown. Remove from pan.

In small bowl, combine cream cheese, remaining 1 tablespoon sugar, orange juice and peel until well blended. Cover and chill. Serve with muffins.

Makes 12 muffins

*Light PHILADELPHIA BRAND® Neufchâtel Cheese may be substituted.

Orange Coconut Muffins

¾ cup all-purpose flour
¾ cup whole wheat flour
⅔ cup toasted wheat germ
½ cup sugar
½ cup coconut
1½ teaspoons baking soda

½ teaspoon salt
1 cup dairy sour cream
2 eggs
1 can (11 ounces) mandarin
    oranges, drained
½ cup chopped nuts

In large bowl, combine flours, wheat germ, sugar, coconut, baking soda and salt. In small bowl, blend sour cream, eggs and oranges. Stir into flour mixture just until moistened. Fold in nuts. Spoon into buttered 2½-inch muffin cups, filling ¾ full. Bake in preheated 400° oven 18 to 20 minutes or until wooden pick inserted in center comes out clean. Remove from pan. Cool on wire rack.

Makes about 12 muffins

Favorite recipe from **Wisconsin Milk Marketing Board© 1989**

Black Cherry Muffins

2 cups all-purpose flour
1 tablespoon baking powder
¼ teaspoon salt
1 cup pitted black cherries, coarsely
    chopped
6 tablespoons butter or margarine,
    softened

⅔ cup sugar
2 eggs
1 teaspoon vanilla
½ cup milk

Preheat oven to 400°. Grease or paper-line 12 (2½-inch) muffin cups. In small bowl, combine flour, baking powder and salt. Toss 1 tablespoon of the flour mixture with the cherries; set aside. In large bowl, beat butter and sugar until light and fluffy. Add eggs and vanilla; beat 3 minutes. Alternately beat in flour mixture and the milk. Fold in cherries. Spoon into muffin cups. Bake 20 to 25 minutes or until golden and wooden pick inserted in center comes out clean. Remove from pan. Cool on wire rack.

Makes 12 muffins

Orange Coconut Muffins

Cranberry-Apricot Tea Cakes

Cranberry-Apricot Tea Cakes

1¼ cups boiling water
¾ cup dried apricots
½ cup butter or margarine, softened
¾ cup granulated sugar
2 eggs
1½ teaspoons vanilla
1¾ cups all-purpose flour
2 teaspoons baking powder
½ teaspoon baking soda

½ teaspoon salt
1 cup OCEAN SPRAY® fresh or frozen Cranberries, coarsely chopped
½ cup chopped nuts
Powdered sugar, for garnish
OCEAN SPRAY® Cranberries, for garnish

In medium bowl, pour boiling water over apricots; let soak 15 minutes to soften. Drain, reserving ¾ cup of the liquid. Coarsely chop apricots; set aside.

Preheat oven to 375°. Grease and flour or paper-line 2½-inch muffin cups. In large bowl, cream butter and granulated sugar until light and fluffy. Beat in eggs, one at a time, until well blended; beat in vanilla. In medium bowl, sift together flour, baking powder, baking soda and salt. With mixer on low speed, alternately add flour mixture and the ¾ cup apricot soaking liquid to the butter mixture, beating well after each addition. Fold in chopped cranberries, chopped apricots and nuts. Spoon batter into muffin cups, filling ¾ full. Bake 20 to 23 minutes or until wooden pick inserted in center comes out clean.

Cool in pan on wire rack 5 minutes. Remove from pan. Dust with powdered sugar. Garnish each tea cake with a whole cranberry, if desired.

Makes about 24 tea cakes

Note: To give as a gift, either return tea cakes to a new muffin pan to include as a gift or arrange in a box or on a gift plate.

Glazed Strawberry Lemon Streusel Muffins

Lemon Streusel Topping (recipe follows)
1½ cups all-purpose flour
½ cup granulated sugar
2 teaspoons baking powder
1 teaspoon ground cinnamon
¼ teaspoon salt
½ cup milk

½ cup butter or margarine, melted
1 egg
1½ cups fresh strawberries, quartered or cut into ½-inch pieces
1 teaspoon grated lemon peel
Lemon Glaze (recipe follows)

Preheat oven to 375°. Paper-line 12 (2½-inch) muffin cups. Prepare Lemon Streusel Topping; set aside.

In large bowl, combine flour, sugar, baking powder, cinnamon and salt. In small bowl, combine milk, butter and egg. Pour into flour mixture, stirring just until moistened. Fold in strawberries and lemon peel. Spoon into muffin cups. Sprinkle Lemon Streusel Topping over batter. Bake 20 to 25 minutes or until wooden pick inserted in center comes out clean. Remove from pan. Prepare Lemon Glaze; drizzle over warm muffins.

Makes 12 muffins

Lemon Streusel Topping: In medium bowl, combine ½ cup chopped pecans, ½ cup packed dark brown sugar, ¼ cup all-purpose flour, 1 teaspoon ground cinnamon and 1 teaspoon grated lemon peel. Add 2 tablespoons melted butter or margarine, stirring until mixture is crumbly.

Lemon Glaze: In small bowl, combine ½ cup powdered sugar and 1 tablespoon fresh lemon juice, stirring until smooth.

Pineapple Citrus Muffins

⅓ cup honey
¼ cup butter or margarine, softened
1 egg
1 can (8 ounces) DOLE® Crushed Pineapple
1 tablespoon grated orange peel
1 cup all-purpose flour

1 cup whole wheat flour
1½ teaspoons baking powder
¼ teaspoon salt
¼ teaspoon ground nutmeg
1 cup DOLE™ Chopped Dates
½ cup DOLE™ Chopped Natural Almonds, toasted

In large bowl, beat honey and butter 1 minute. Beat in egg, then undrained pineapple and orange peel. In medium bowl, combine flours, baking powder, salt, nutmeg, dates and almonds. Stir into pineapple mixture until just moistened. Spoon into greased 2½-inch muffin cups. Bake in 375° oven 25 minutes or until wooden pick inserted in center comes out clean. Remove from pan. Cool on wire rack.

Makes 12 muffins

Acknowledgements

We wish to thank the following organizations and companies for the use of their recipes.

Almond Board of California
American Dairy Association
American Egg Board
Best Foods, a division of CPC International
Borden, Inc.
Checkerboard Kitchens, Ralston Purina Company
Church & Dwight Co., Inc.
Diamond Walnut Growers, Inc.
Dole Packaged Foods Co.
Hershey Foods Corporation
Kraft, Inc.
Libby, Division of Carnation Company
MBG Marketing™
McIlhenny Company, Avery Island, Louisiana 70513
Nabisco Brands, Inc.
National Cherry Foundation
Ocean Spray Cranberries, Inc.
Oklahoma Peanut Commission
The Quaker Oats Company
Roman Meal Company
Swift-Eckrich, Inc.
United Fresh Fruit and Vegetable Association
Western New York Apple Growers Association, Inc.
Wisconsin Milk Marketing Board© 1989

Picture Credits

We wish to thank the following organizations and companies for the use of their photos.

Almond Board of California 26, 87
American Egg Board 14
Borden, Inc. 30, 43, 47, 88
Checkerboard Kitchens, Ralston Purina Company 39
Dole Packaged Foods Co. 7, 21, 52, 60
Hershey Foods Corporation 55, 70, 83
Libby, Division of Carnation Company 25
Nabisco Brands, Inc. 65
National Cherry Foundation 56
Ocean Spray Cranberries, Inc. 92
Swift-Eckrich, Inc. 10, 59

INDEX